IMAGES OF WAR

KOREA
THE GROUND WAR
FROM BOTH SIDES

RARE PHOTOGRAPHS FROM WARTIME ARCHIVES

PHILIP CHINNERY

Pen & Sword
MILITARY

First published in Great Britain in 2013 by
PEN & SWORD MILITARY
An imprint of
Pen & Sword Books Ltd
47 Church Street
Barnsley
South Yorkshire
S70 2AS

ISBN 978-1-84884-819-1

Typeset by Concept, Huddersfield, West Yorkshire
Printed and bound in England by CPI Group (UK) Ltd, Croydon, CR0 4YY.

Pen & Sword Books Ltd incorporates the Imprints of Pen & Sword Aviation,
Pen & Sword Family History, Pen & Sword Maritime, Pen & Sword Military, Pen & Sword Discovery,
Wharncliffe Local History, Wharncliffe True Crime, Wharncliffe Transport, Pen & Sword Select,
Pen & Sword Military Classics, Leo Cooper, The Praetorian Press, Remember When,
Seaforth Publishing and Frontline Publishing.

For a complete list of Pen & Sword titles please contact
PEN & SWORD BOOKS LIMITED
47 Church Street, Barnsley, South Yorkshire, S70 2AS, England
E-mail: enquiries@pen-and-sword.co.uk
Website: www.pen-and-sword.co.uk

Contents

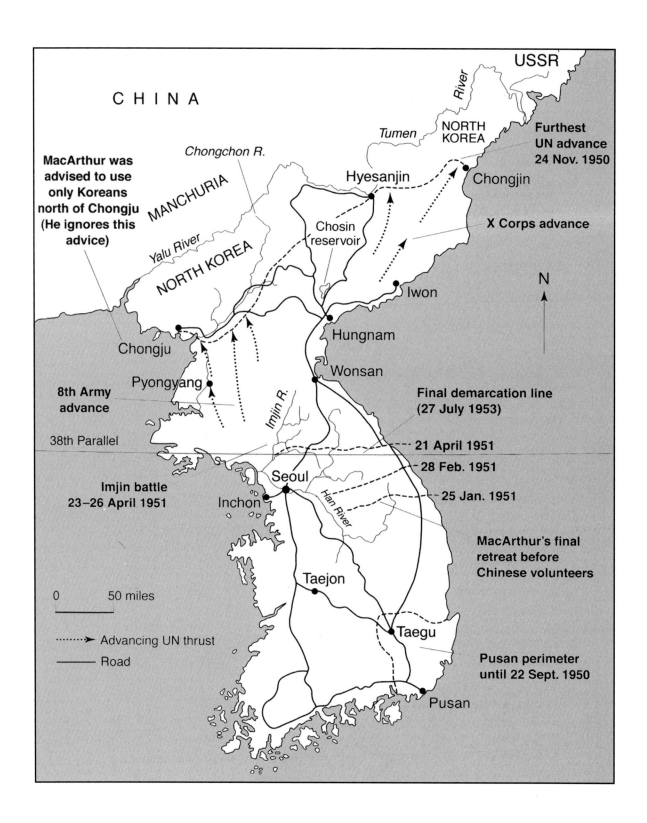

CHINA

MacArthur was advised to use only Koreans north of Chongju (He ignores this advice)

MANCHURIA

Chongchon R.

Yalu River

NORTH KOREA

USSR

Tumen

River

NORTH KOREA

Hyesanjin

Chosin reservoir

Furthest UN advance 24 Nov. 1950

Chongjin

X Corps advance

Iwon

N

Hungnam

Chongju

8th Army advance

Pyongyang

Wonsan

Final demarcation line (27 July 1953)

Imjin R.

38th Parallel

21 April 1951

28 Feb. 1951

Imjin battle 23–26 April 1951

Seoul

Inchon

Han River

25 Jan. 1951

MacArthur's final retreat before Chinese volunteers

0   50 miles

Taejon

Taegu

·····► Advancing UN thrust

Road

Pusan perimeter until 22 Sept. 1950

Pusan

Introduction

This book is my third on the subject of the Korean War and is aimed at telling the story of the ground war from the view of both participants: the Communists (North Korea, China and the Soviet Union) and the United Nations (South Korea, United States and the Allied Nations).

The Korean War of 1950–53 was a war of heavy casualties and much suffering. When the Chinese joined the war five months after it began, they employed human wave tactics which were often very successful but very costly in terms of manpower. The American GI on the other hand, was out of his depth in Korea; young, inexperienced in the art of war and initially poorly equipped, thousands perished on the battlefield and many hundreds more surrendered, only to succumb to the harsh conditions in the prisoner of war camps.

Hundreds of thousands of civilians were made homeless by the fighting which swept up and down the peninsula and their plight was pitiful. Trudging along in all weathers, seeking food and shelter, they were pushed off the main roads by the military and often killed at random by North or South Korean troops or Police if they were suspected of being sympathetic to either side. The United States was responsible for a large part of the refugee problem, with their indiscriminate bombing campaigns which laid many towns and cities to waste.

The Communists on the other hand, would force civilians and captured South Korean soldiers to join the ranks of their depleted divisions and then drive them into battle. They had employed the Soviet system of using commissars to drive the infantry forward, with a bullet waiting for any soldier who tried to turn around and retreat. They would be used as cannon fodder, to die in droves while the enemy used up his ammunition thus clearing the way for the better armed and experienced troops to overrun the enemy positions.

We will compare the tactics used by both sides and the weapons that they used: the Americans who would abandon huge amounts of supplies and vehicles on the battlefield and the Chinese who went into battle with weapons captured from the Japanese during the Second World War.

Rations played an important part in the success of the campaigns. The UN troops were well fed, whereas the Chinese carried dry rations and never more than enough for four or five days' fighting. The Americans used vast fleets of trucks and transport aircraft to move their supplies around; the Chinese generally carried theirs on their backs or by pack horses.

The treatment of prisoners on both sides of the fence could not have been more different. The Chinese were not expecting the large number of prisoners that fell into their hands and in the early days did not have the ability to feed or house them. Hundreds died on the march or in the camps during the first year of the war. In the South, thousands of Chinese prisoners had originally fought for the Chinese Nationalists in the civil war and had been taken prisoner and conscripted into the Chinese Army. Now, given the opportunity, they would prefer to go to Formosa rather than back to China.

Photographs taken during the war by South and North Korean photographers are few and far between. Photos taken by Chinese photographers are more easily sourced, but the quality varies and most are taken from a propaganda point of view. The United Nations forces, principally the United States, had plenty of photographers and the quantity and quality of available material far exceeds that of the Communist side.

The reader is asked to accept what is available and to appreciate this effort to illustrate both sides of the Korean War. It was a war of a type that will hopefully not occur again, but with a belligerent government still in control in North Korea, the possibility of a return to those awful days is still on the cards.

Philip Chinnery
East Sussex 2012

Chapter One

On the Verge of Defeat

June – September 1950

Following the defeat of the Japanese and the end of the Second World War, the Korean peninsula had been occupied in the North by the Soviet Union and in the South by the United States. The two halves of the country were partitioned at the 38th Parallel. In 1948 the Republic of Korea was established in the South, ruled by Syngman Rhee whose declared objective was the reunification of Korea as a non-communist state. A month later the Democratic Peoples Republic of Korea was established in the North, led by Kim Il Sung. Elections should have been held to reunite the country, but never took place. By 1949 American combat forces had withdrawn from Korea, but left a military advisor group to assist the ROK army. The Soviet Union however, took an active role in governing North Korea and in early 1950 supplied weapons and several thousand soldiers to train the North Korean Army. Armed clashes were common along the 38th Parallel, but in 1950 US observers did not anticipate an invasion of the South. In January 1950 US Secretary of State Dean Acheson announced an American defensive strategy in the Far East that excluded both Korea and the Nationalist Chinese island of Formosa. It sent a clear signal to the DPRK that Syngman Rhee was on his own.

Colonel Paik Sun Yup was fast asleep when the telephone rang. His breathless G-3 was at the other end: 'The North Koreans have invaded! They're attacking all along the parallel! The situation in Kaesong is chaotic, and I'm afraid the city already may have fallen.' It was 0700 hours on Sunday, 25 June 1950. Colonel Paik was the commander of the 1st Republic of Korea (ROK) Division, protector of Seoul, the capital of South Korea. He was twenty-nine years old. He was also away from his 10,000-man division, on a senior officer training course at the Infantry School in Seoul.

By the time Paik rejoined his division they were in contact with the 1st North Korean Division supported by tanks from the 105th Armoured Brigade. The 1st ROK Division was at the western end of the four divisions tasked with defending the 240 mile long imaginary line which was known as the 38th Parallel and formed the frontier between the two countries. Their section of the line was fifty-six miles long and impossible to defend, so Paik reduced it to nineteen miles by establishing his defences along the Imjin River. However, this meant that Kaesong was left open to the invaders and it fell within hours, with the 12th Regiment falling back in disarray.

The 13th Regiment at Munsan was also involved in a pitched battle and the third regiment of the division, the 11th was called up from its reserve position. However, 50 per cent of its personnel were on leave and it would take time for the men to rejoin their unit.

The 7th ROK Division was established to the east of the 1st ROK Division, but communications had broken down and their present situation was unknown.

At the time of the invasion, South Korea possessed eight infantry divisions and four of them – 1st, 6th, 7th and 8th – were in position along the 38th Parallel. They were armed with American M1 rifles, 0.30-calibre carbines, 60mm and 81mm mortars, 2.36-inch rocket launchers and the M3 105mm howitzers. They had no tanks, no medium artillery and no fighter aircraft or bombers.

The North Korean Army that attacked the South consisted of ten infantry divisions, eight of them at full strength with 11,000 men each plus one armoured brigade equipped with Russian T-34 tanks mounting an 85mm gun, an armoured regiment and two independent regiments totalling 135,000 men. They were equipped with 150 tanks, over 600 artillery pieces and 196 aircraft, including forty fighters and seventy bombers. Of the ten divisions, three were former Chinese Communist 4th Field Army divisions, 38,000 ethnic Koreans who had fought on the communist side during the Chinese civil war, so they were combat-hardened and efficient. The North Koreans had spent over 13.8 million rubles to purchase Soviet weaponry including 76mm and 122mm howitzers, 45mm anti-aircraft guns and 82mm and 120mm mortars. The invasion force comprised two Corps, both commanded by Koreans who had fought for Mao Zedung in the Chinese civil war. The commanders of the 5th, 6th and 7th Divisions were all veterans of the Chinese 4th Field Army and their men all brought their weapons with them when they crossed the Yalu River back into North Korea.

During the afternoon of 25 June, North Korean aircraft attacked South Korean and United States Air Force aircraft and facilities at Seoul airfield and Kimpo air base, just south of Seoul. They left a C-54 transport aircraft burning at Kimpo and one of its crew became the first American to be wounded in the Korean War.

The next day US Far East Air Force fighters based in Japan flew top cover while ships began to evacuate American citizens from Inchon, a seaport on the Yellow Sea, twenty miles west of Seoul. On the following day, 27 June, the UN Defensive Campaign formally commenced when Fifth Air Force fighters destroyed three North Korean Yak fighters, the first aerial victories of the war. The UN Defensive Campaign was the first of ten campaigns that would be fought the length and breadth of the

Korean Peninsula over the next three years and the participants would be awarded medals accordingly.

As the North Koreans began to push the ROK forces southwards and Seoul fell to the invaders, the United Nations voted to assist the Republic of Korea. The United States would take the lead and President Harry S. Truman ordered US air and naval forces to help counter the invasion. Within days advance elements of the US 24th Infantry Division were on their way from Japan to the port of Pusan in the south-east corner of the peninsula. The men were part of the occupation forces that had been in Japan for the last five years and they were inadequately trained, poorly armed and led by inexperienced officers.

A small combat team from 1st Battalion, 21st Infantry Regiment was flown in to try to slow the North Korean advance. However, by the time Task Force Smith had arrived at Pusan airfield and boarded trucks for the drive northwards, the North Koreans had crossed the Han River and taken Suwon and were already on the way toward their next objective: Taejon.

Lieutenant Colonel Charles Smith and his 400 men moved into their positions about eight miles south of Suwon, where the road ran through a saddle of hills. Supported by six 105mm howitzers and 140 artillerymen they dug in and waited with trepidation for the enemy to appear. At 0730 hours on 5 July the North Korean column came in sight, led by thirty-three T-34 tanks, spearheading the advance of the 4th Division. They were engaged by the howitzers, then the recoilless rifles and bazookas of the infantry. However, none of them managed to penetrate the armour on the tanks and by 0900 hours they had driven down the road and past the defenders. It would be another week before the first large 3.5-inch bazookas and their larger and more destructive shaped charges arrived from the United States. Now the main column came into view, led by three more tanks and when they got closer Smith ordered his men to open fire with mortars and machine guns. The North Koreans quickly disembarked and instead of attacking the defenders head on, began to outflank them. The artillery managed to destroy two of the tanks with anti-tank rounds, but as they only had six of them they did not last long. The normal high-explosive rounds simply ricocheted off the sides of the tanks. Anti-tank mines would have stopped the T-34s but there were none in Korea at that time.

At 1430 hours Smith ordered his men to withdraw, but the withdrawal was disorganised and nearly all the heavy weapons and twenty-five wounded men were left behind. Intense enemy fire caused heavy casualties amongst the GIs and only half of them made it back to safety; the rest were either killed or captured. In the meantime Major-General Dean, the commander of the division had arrived at Pusan and he sent the 34th Infantry Regiment up to P'yongt'aek with orders to hold the line. Lieutenant Colonel Loveless had only been in command of the 34th for a month. He had been brought in to replace the previous commander, who had failed to improve the fighting qualities of the regiment. Not only were the companies under strength, with about 140 officers and men each, but their weapons were inadequate as well. Each man had either an M1 or a carbine with 80 or 100 rounds of ammunition – enough for about ten minutes of firing. There were no hand grenades either, essential items for close-quarter fighting. A third of the officers had seen combat during the Second World War, but only one in six of the enlisted men had any experience of combat. The rest were at best only semi-trained and averaged under twenty years of age.

The men of the 1st Battalion stood in their water logged trenches until dawn broke. They had earlier been told that Task Force Smith had been defeated and in the early hours they had heard the sound of the bridge behind them being destroyed, to prevent its use by tanks. It was bad for morale and when dawn broke and they saw a line of tanks and trucks extending as far as the eye could see, they were ready to run. They were also without artillery support and when the first tank shells began to explode around them, they climbed out of their foxholes and began to retreat back to P'yongt'aek.

The poor performance of the American soldiers was due to the post-war complacency of their commanders and hundreds would die because of it. In this case the 34th Infantry Regiment was a third under strength and the two battalions were ill equipped and poorly trained for the battles ahead. The blame for this went right to the top, from the divisions officers, to General Dean and the commander of the US Eighth Army General Walton Walker. Ultimately the buck stopped at the desk of General MacArthur whose primary concern at that time was the rehabilitation of Japanese society and that country's economy.

General Walker's advance party established the headquarters of the US Eighth Army at Taegu on 9 July and the next day the 25th Infantry Division began to arrive. To the east of the country the South Koreans were carrying out a fighting retreat to prevent the enemy from outflanking the American forces. As the North Korean 3rd and 4th Divisions prepared to cross the Kum River and advance on Taejon, General Dean marshaled his forces to oppose them. The 4th Division was at half strength with 6,000 fighting men, but they also had fifty tanks. The 3rd Division had no tanks, but was up to full strength. The US 24th Infantry Division had 11,000 men on its strength, but there were only 5,300 at the sharp end. It would be a hard fought battle.

On 19 July General Dean and the three regiments of the 24th Division prepared to defend Taejon. General Walker told him that he had to hold the town for at least two days, to allow the 25th Division and the 1st Cavalry Division to reach the front. It was easier said than done. The enemy had rebuilt the bridge over the Kum River, ten miles north of Taejon and started to move tanks and artillery across. By midnight the two enemy divisions had encircled the town and were establishing roadblocks to the south and east. General Dean and his aide had spent the night in Taejon and awoke to the sound of small arms fire. Amazingly, considering his heavy responsibilities, the General found a pair of bazooka teams and went out tank hunting. By the afternoon of 20 July, General Dean realized that the battle was lost and ordered the withdrawal of the remaining units. Towards evening the main convoy tried to leave the town but came under enemy fire. General Dean's jeep took a wrong turning and soon came under fire. After sheltering for a while in a ditch, Dean and his party made it to the banks of the Taejon River. They hid there until dark and then tried to climb the mountain north of the village of Nangwol.

Sergeant George Libby was in a truck which was hit by devastating enemy fire which killed or wounded all on board except Libby. He administered first aid to his comrades and flagged down a passing M5 artillery tractor and helped the wounded aboard. The enemy opened fire on the vehicle and Libby, realizing that no one else could operate the tractor, placed himself between the driver and the enemy, thereby shielding him while he returned the fire. Although wounded several times, Libby stopped to pick up more wounded and continued to shield the driver and return fire as they approached another roadblock. He sustained further wounds and died as his comrades reached friendly lines. For his courage and self-sacrifice he was posthumously awarded the Medal of Honour.

As darkness fell on the hills around Taejon General Dean and his party paused for a rest. Dean decided to go off on his own to look for water for the wounded, but he fell down a steep slope and was knocked out. When he came to, he discovered he had a broken shoulder and was disoriented. Up above, the rest of the party waited for two more hours for Dean to reappear, then set off for the American lines. General Dean spent thirty-six long days wandering the countryside before he was betrayed by two civilians and captured. His weight had dropped from 190 to 130 pounds and he was to spend the rest of the war in solitary confinement. If that was not bad enough, almost 1,200 of his men had become casualties.

Towards the end of July an incident took place that would lead to a review by the Department of the Army Inspector General fifty years later. Korean villagers stated that on 25 July 1950, US soldiers evacuated approximately 500 to 600 villagers from their homes in Im Gae Ri and Joo Gok Ri. The villagers said the US soldiers escorted them towards the south. Later that evening, the American soldiers led the villagers near a riverbank at Ha Ga Ri and ordered them to stay there that night. During the night, the villagers witnessed a long parade of US troops and vehicles moving towards Pusan.

On the morning of 26 July, the villagers continued south along the Seoul-Pusan road. According to their statements, when the villagers reached the vicinity of No Gun Ri, US soldiers stopped them at a roadblock and ordered the group onto the railroad tracks, where soldiers searched them and their personal belongings. The Koreans state that, although the soldiers found no prohibited articles such as weapons or other military contraband, the soldiers ordered an air attack upon the villagers via radio communications with US aircraft. Shortly afterwards, planes flew over and dropped bombs and fired machine guns, killing approximately 100 villagers on the railroad tracks. Those villagers who survived sought protection in a small culvert underneath the railroad tracks. The US soldiers drove the villagers out of the culvert and into the larger double tunnels nearby. The Koreans state that the US soldiers then fired into both ends of the tunnels over a period of four days (26–29 July 1950), resulting in approximately 300 additional deaths.

At the time of the incident, the South Koreans and their American allies were retreating before the North Korean advance. The roads were packed with refugees and amongst them were North Korean infiltrators. The US Divisional commanders had given orders to keep the refugees off the roads and generally relied on the Korean National Police to carry out the work. Sometimes they were too enthusiastic and shot civilians considered to be Communist sympathizers or infiltrators. Major General Gay, the 1st Cavalry Division Commander was alleged to have commented that he would not employ the National Police in his division's area of operations. However, such decisions were being taken by higher authorities.

On 26 July, the Eighth Army in coordination with the ROK government formulated a plan to control the movement of refugees, which precluded the movement of refugees across battle lines at all times, prohibited evacuation of villages without general officer approval and prescribed procedures for the Korean National Police to clear desired areas and routes. They also strictly precluded the movement of civilians during the hours of darkness.

It was under these conditions that the above incident took place. The 5th and 7th Cavalry Regiments were withdrawing through the area at the time. An enemy break-through was reported in the sector to the north of the 7th Cavalry position and in the early hours of 26 July their 2nd Battalion conducted a disorganized and undisciplined withdrawal to the vicinity of No Gun Ri. They spent the remaining hours of 26 July until late into that night recovering abandoned personnel and equipment from the area where the air strike and machine gun firing on Korean refugees is alleged to have occurred. By that night 119 men were still unaccounted for.

The 7th Cavalry relieved the 2nd Battalion in the afternoon of 26 July and reported an enemy column on the railroad tracks on the 27th, which they fired upon. On the 29th they withdrew as the North Koreans advanced, so for two days they had believed they were under attack. It was later proven that the Air Force were strafing to the south-west of No Gun Ri on 27 July, but they were mistakenly strafing the command post of the 1st Battalion of the 7th Cavalry, rather than the enemy. It was not the first instance of 'friendly fire' and it certainly would not be the last.

Were the cavalrymen responsible for the civilian casualties? The review in 2001 could not establish for sure. However, the fact is that the American troops had been thrown into action straight from occupation duty in Japan, mostly without training for, or experience in combat. They were young, under-trained and unprepared for the fight they would wage against the North Korean Peoples Army. Many of their NCOs had been transferred to the 24th US Infantry Division and they were facing a determined assault by a well-armed and well-trained enemy employing both conventional and guerilla warfare tactics. In these circumstances some soldiers may have fired in response to a perceived enemy threat without considering the possibility that they may be civilians.

By 5 August, the North Korean advance had ground to a halt, due to a combination of factors: air attacks by the Far East Air Forces, lengthening supply lines and stiffer resistance from the South Korean Army and the United States troops who were now arriving in force. The defenders were now occupying only the south-east portion of the country, in a forty- to sixty-mile arc around the sea port of Pusan.

Another Medal of Honour would be awarded to Sergeant Ernest Kouma for his actions on 31 August and 1 September. The 2nd US Infantry Division had just replaced the battle-weary 24th Division when the North Koreans began to cross the Naktong River under cover of darkness. As they did so, Sergeant Kouma led his patrol of two M26 Pershing tanks and two M19 Gun Motor Carriages along the river bank to the Kihang Ferry near Agok. A heavy fog covered the river and at 2200 hours mortar shells began falling on the American-held side of the river. When the fog lifted half an hour later Kouma saw that a North Korean pontoon bridge was being laid across the river directly in front of his position. The four vehicles opened fire and sank many of the boats trying to cross the river. Kouma was manning the M2 0.50-calibre Browning machine gun in the tank turret when he was told over the field telephone that the supporting infantry were withdrawing. He decided to act as rearguard to cover the infantry and was shot in the foot shortly thereafter while reloading the tank's ammunition. His force was then ambushed by a group of North Koreans dressed in US military uniforms. Kouma was wounded in the shoulder as he repeatedly beat back the attacking North Koreans. Eventually the other three vehicles withdrew or were knocked out and Kouma held the crossing site until 0730 hours the next morning. At one point the tank was surrounded and out of ammunition for its main gun and Kouma held them off with his machine gun, pistol and grenades. The tank then withdrew eight miles to the newly-established American lines, destroying three North Korean machine gun positions along the way. During this action Kouma had killed an estimated 250 North Korean troops.

The defenders of the Pusan Perimeter would try to keep the enemy at bay while General MacArthur planned the second US campaign of the war: the UN Offensive Campaign, which would last from 16 September until 2 November 1950.

The US Defensive Campaign ended on 15 September. The following day the fight back began with Operation Chromite, a daring amphibious landing at Inchon, a port on the west coast of Korea and far behind the enemy lines. The X Corps invasion force, numbering nearly 70,000 men, arrived off the beaches 150 miles behind enemy lines. It was the first major amphibious assault by American troops since Okinawa in April 1945. After a three hour naval bombardment, the men of the First Marine Division began to disembark from their landing craft at 0633 hours on the fortified Wolmi Island that protected Inchon harbour. It was defended by 400 men of the North Korean 226th Independent Marine Regiment, but by 0750 hours the island was in the hands of the US Marines. Because of the high tides, the landing on the Inchon shoreline did not take place until the afternoon when the 1st and 5th Marines approached Red and Blue Beaches at 1733 hours. Most of the men had to scale the seawall with scaling ladders before assaulting the two objectives in front of them: the Cemetery and Observatory Hills. By midnight the beachhead was secure at the cost of twenty Marines killed and 174 wounded. In the morning the two Marine regiments began to move inland, driving the North Koreans before them. The 7th Infantry Division would begin to land at Inchon the following day as the 5th Marines began its drive towards Kimpo airfield. The first Marine aircraft began to fly sorties from the field on the 21st. The enemy suffered heavy losses that day, trying to cross the Han River into Seoul. They were caught in the open with nowhere to hide and the Marine Corsairs made run after run on them, with napalm, bombs, rockets and 20mm cannon.

The Air Force's contribution to the invasion was Air Interdiction Campaign No. 2, the first objective of which was to limit the flow of reinforcements to the landing zone at Inchon. The FEAF B-29s would also have to hit the rail yard at Seoul in the days before the landing and General MacArthur made it clear that he would require heavy air support for Eighth Army as it broke out of the Pusan Perimeter in pursuit of the North Koreans.

The Eighth Army had been reorganized into I Corps and IX Corps. The most reliable units were allocated to I Corps: the 5th Regimental Combat Team, the 1st Cavalry Division, the rebuilt 24th Division, the 27th British Commonwealth Brigade and the South Koreans' best division, the 1st ROK Division. They were to break out of the Pusan Perimeter and spearhead the 180-mile drive north to meet up with Major General Almonds X Corps which was coming ashore at Inchon. IX Corps and its 2nd and 25th US Divisions would follow on a week later. On the east side of the country the ROK I and II Corps were to engage the enemy the best they could.

The breakout of Eighth Army was to begin on 16 September with a force of eighty-two B-29s bombing a pathway along the line Taegu-Taejon-Suwon. However, the weather delayed the attacks until 18 September when forty-two B-29s started to clear a path for the 38th Infantry Regiment to cross the Naktong River. This was followed by 286 close air support sorties from F-51s, F-80s and B-26s. A further 361 were flown the next day, halting North Korean counter attacks and weakening their defences until, on 22 September, the North Korean Army collapsed, leaving the door open for a race to the 38th Parallel.

Bomber Command pursued the retreating North Koreans and attacked them by day and night. The B-29s had been practising dropping flares at night, so that B-26s could attack the targets illuminated by the flares. On 22 September the roving B-26s bombed and strafed a long North Korean ammunition train south of Suwon and the explosions went on for an hour. Other B-29s flew psychological warfare missions dropping leaflets over retreating North Korean columns. Many prisoners surrendered with these leaflets in their hands.

As the bombing effort switched from the south to the north, the B-29s ranged far and wide looking for new targets. On 22 September a B-29 from the 98th Bomb Group spotted a town with a rail marshalling yard and bombed it. Several days passed before the Air Force managed to identify the town and discovered that it was actually Antung, across the Yalu River in Chinese Manchuria. The warning to stay clear of the Chinese border went out to the bomber crews and four days later attacks began against the North Korean hydro-electric plants, the first target for the 92nd Bomb Group being the electric plant at Hungnam. On the same day, UN forces fought their way into Seoul and began four days of street to street fighting to evict the 20,000 North Korean defenders. When Seoul finally fell on 28 September the total US casualties for the Inchon-Seoul operations had reached 3,500. Enemy casualties were estimated at 14,000 killed and 7,000 captured.

On 27 September, MacArthur received authorization from the Joint Chiefs to send his forces across the border into North Korea and on 1 October all bombing in South Korea ceased. The same day the first South Koreans crossed the 38th Parallel, heading north. By now there were four US Army Divisions and a Marine Division in action. The first major Allied contingent had arrived in the shape of the 27th British Commonwealth Brigade and the 90,000 ROK troops were now receiving the weapons and training they sorely needed two months earlier.

On 7 October the UN General Assembly approved a US-sponsored motion that stability be restored on the Korean Peninsula, by defeating the North Korean forces and restoring democracy to both sides of the border. MacArthur met President Truman at Wake Island a week later and informed him, although there were intelligence reports of Chinese forces massing across the border, he considered it safe to pursue the North Koreans right up to the Yalu River.

In the meantime the Marines had been recalled to their ships and had sailed south around the bottom of the peninsula and up the east coast to the port of Wonsan. By the time the Navy had cleared the enemy mines from the harbour and the Marines had come ashore, the UN forces had swept past the town with the enemy in full retreat. The race for the North Korean capital of P'yongyang was under way. Three ROK divisions were driving northwards, together with the US 1st Cavalry Division, the 24th Division and the 27th British Commonwealth Brigade. On 19 October units of the 5th Cavalry entered P'yongyang, just minutes ahead of the ROK 1st Division. With the fall of their capital, North Korean resistance began to increase. On 20 October, 2,860 paratroopers from the 187th Regimental Combat Team and 300 tons of supplies were dropped near Sukchon and Sunchon, thirty miles north-east of P'yongyang. One of their objectives was to halt two North Korean trains full of American prisoners of war that were heading for POW camps along the Yalu River. They arrived too late and found that many of the prisoners had been murdered by their guards at the side of the railroad tracks.

At the same time Fifth Air Force began reporting increased enemy air attacks along the border. The new Russian Mig-15 fighter had made its debut, flown by Russian and Chinese pilots and it outclassed all other jets being flown by UN squadrons at that time. MacArthur wanted bombing missions flown against the bridges crossing the Yalu River, to prevent supplies coming in to North Korea and to block the path of retreat for the North Koreans into Manchuria. However, at the time the Air Force was prohibited from flying within five miles of the Manchurian border.

Originally, the Joint Chiefs only approved the use of South Korean units north of the 38th Parallel, but MacArthur ordered all of his forces to advance with all possible speed. He was taking a considerable risk and did not fully appreciate the possible reaction of the Soviets and Chinese as the UN forces approached their borders. On 26 October, advance units of the 6th Division of the ROK III Corps reached the Yalu River. Over the radio came the first reports that they had killed a small number of Chinese troops. At the same time the ROK 1st Division captured Chinese prisoners at Sudong. The next day, 27 October, the Chinese first-phase offensive was launched.

Two South Korean officers survey the area north of the border before the start of the invasion. Korea had been partitioned at the end of the Second World War along the 38th Parallel.

A North Korean tank regiment prepares to advance. They were equipped with the Russian built T-34 tank, which had proven itself against the German Army in the Second World War.

North Korean light artillery open fire with Soviet 76mm M1927/39 regimental guns on the thinly-spread defenders of Seoul.

North Korean T-34 tanks rumble into Seoul as communist sympathizers celebrate their arrival.

A poor quality, but extremely rare photograph of North Korean troops entering the outskirts of Seoul.

North Korean forces entered Seoul only three days after the start of the invasion. A third of the invasion army had fought in the Chinese civil war and were battle-hardened veterans.

General MacArthur arrives in his personal C-54 'Bataan'. After a brief visit to assess the situation he returned to Japan and recommended the deployment of United States infantry divisions to bolster the South Korean Army.

The lightly armed Republic of Korea (ROK) troops were no match for the tanks and artillery of their northern neighbour and they retreated in disarray.

North Korean leader Kim Il Sung visiting North Korean tank crews, following the capture of Seoul. The young leader erroneously thought that the South Koreans would rise up and support the invaders.

US troops arrive at the dockside in Pusan, 6 August 1950. The men of the 24th Infantry Division were inexperienced and poorly armed and did little to slow the North Korean advance.

Infantry from the all-black 24th Infantry Regiment moving up to the front on 18 July 1950. This segregated unit, led by white officers performed badly and was later disbanded.

American troops from the 24th Infantry Division arriving at Taejon railway station. They would be no match for the North Koreans who would drive them out within twenty-four hours.

American prisoners of war taken in the early months of the war were treated very badly by their North Korean captors. This photo was taken by the communists and shows exhausted prisoners trying to rest whilst piled one on top of the other. They were given little food or water and medical treatment was non-existent. Many died on the march to the camps in the North.

One of four Americans from the 21st Infantry Regiment, 24th Infantry Division found murdered between their forward observation post and the front line on 10 July 1950. Captured the previous night, they had been tied up and shot in the head.

The reality of war – an American NCO surveys the dead scattered around a hilltop.

British troops arrive with the 27th British Commonwealth Brigade. The soldier on the right is a radioman Private Clem Williams and the one on the left with the binoculars is Sergeant Derrick Deamer.

North Korean troops advancing. Their officers are wearing the darker uniforms and many held posts in the Chinese 4th Field Army during the Chinese civil war. The soldiers are armed with Soviet PPSh-41 SMGs fitted with the smaller and lighter 35-round curved magazine that first appeared in 1942. It made reloading easier than the clumsier 71-round drum magazine.

A 75mm M20 recoilless rifle is ready to fire as the assistant waits with the next shell. Note the field telephone on the sandbag to the left of the gunner, ready to relay targets to the gun crew. Its shaped charge warhead was capable of penetrating 100mm of armour, although it was used primarily as a close infantry support weapon.

A 105mm howitzer in action. The build up of US forces continued in the Pusan Perimeter while General MacArthur planned an amphibious landing on the west coast of Korea.

A wounded Marine is helped away for treatment on the Naktong River front.

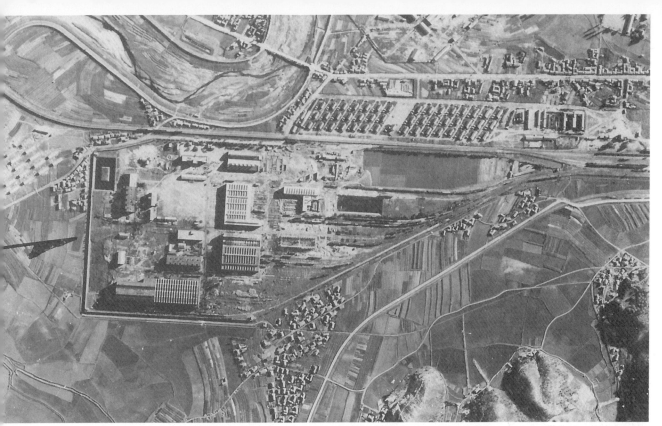

A before and after photograph of a B-29 bombing raid on the railway yards at Wonsan on 24 August 1950. UN air power helped slow the North Korean advance down towards the southern tip of the peninsula and the port of Pusan.

The first American soldiers to arrive in Korea were woefully equipped and poorly trained. They were killed and captured in their hundreds. This young soldier is holding his rifle with bayonet fixed. Note he has not fitted the magazine.

12 July 1950, photographs of well-camouflaged American vehicles are seldom seen. This may have been a command post in a South Korean village.

Until the arrival of the 3.5-inch bazooka (shown above), American troops had no weapons at company level to combat the North Korean T-34 tanks. During the first months of the war they had to use the 2.36-inch version which had little effect on the enemy armour.

A T-34 tank destroyed by a 3.5-inch bazooka team from the US 24th Infantry Division near Taejon. General Dean was taken prisoner after the battle and spent the rest of the war in solitary confinement. Note that the drive sprocket (at the rear) has been shot off.

In July 1950 the few fighters of the North Korean Air Force were still roaming the skies in the South. Here an American tank crewman searches the sky from his camouflaged M24 Chaffee light tank.

Camouflaged North Korean T34 tanks and motor cycle combinations enter Taejon city after the eviction of the US 24th Infantry Division.

A recently declassified photograph showing the execution of 1,800 South Korean political prisoners in Taejon over three days in July 1950. The retreating South Korean Army feared that the suspected communist sympathizers might collaborate with the advancing North Koreans. Both sides routinely executed citizens and soldiers alike as the fighting continued.

On the Pusan Perimeter, 26 August 1950. Men of the 7th Regiment, 1st Cavalry Division fire their 0.50-calibre machine gun at North Korean troops on the north bank of the Naktong River.

Sergeant Ernest Kouma was awarded the Medal of Honour for his actions at the Naktong River as the North Koreans forced a crossing. This tank commander is firing his 0.50-calibre machine gun, the same as was mounted on Kouma's tank.

Letcher V. Gardner from 'D' Company, 1st Cavalry Division fires on a North Korean emplacement along the Naktong River near Chingu on 13 August 1950.

Marine M46 Patton tank is resupplied with fuel and ammunition in the Pusan Perimeter.

Troops of the 5th Cavalry inspect a North Korean T-34 tank knocked out near Waegwan on 20 September 1950. It belonged to the North Korean 16th Armoured Brigade which was largely destroyed in the Naktong fighting.

Private Julias Van Den Stock of 'A' Company, 32nd Regimental Combat Team, 7th Infantry Division rests on an enemy bunker next to a Soviet DP light machine gun along the slope of Hill 902 north of Ip-Tong.

The break out from the Pusan Perimeter. M26 Pershings of 72nd Tank Battalion with infantry of the 2nd Infantry Division at Yongsan on 3 September 1950.

Jeeps and trucks from the US 24th Infantry Division cross the Naktong River to begin the drive north.

A 105mm howitzer crew from the US 25th Infantry Division strip to the waist as they send hundreds of shells towards the North Korean lines near Uirson on 27 August 1950.

Finally equipped with heavier weapons, these South Korean troops are manhandling their camouflaged howitzer into position.

Two North Korean prisoners of war ride on the hood of this US 2nd Infantry Division jeep after being taken prisoner in the fighting for Yongsan on 2 September 1950. They are being taken to the rear in the Naktong River sector of the Pusan Perimeter.

A bailey bridge is constructed over a destroyed road bridge near the Naktong River. A North Korean T-34 tank was hiding under the bridge when it was destroyed by air attack.

The bodies of these murdered American soldiers were recovered as the UN forces pushed north out of the Pusan Perimeter. They were all killed while their hands were bound behind their backs.

Men from the US 2nd Infantry Division probe for mines along the road through this village as they advance from Changnyong, south of Taegu towards the Naktong River.

14 September 1950, engineers probe for a booby trap underneath a communist mine near Haman, South Korea.

North Korean tank crewmen lie dead next to their two Soviet T-34 tanks at Indong, north of Waegwan, possibly destroyed by Mustang fighters from the Royal Australian Air Force on 13 August 1950.

Two knocked out North Korean tanks, pushed off the road by the advancing UN forces.

Operation Chromite begins early in the morning of 15 September 1950. Landing craft carrying the 1st Marine Division head towards Inchon as battleships fire on targets pinpointed by the Marines' own close support aircraft.

15 September 1951, Marines scrambling up the harbour wall at Inchon. This platoon was led by Lieutenant Baldomero Lopez who was killed minutes later when smothering a live grenade with his body. He was posthumously awarded the Medal of Honour.

Four LSTs unload on the beach at Inchon as Marines gather equipment to move rapidly inland on 15 September 1950. The landing ships were stuck in the deep mud flats between one high tide and the next.

US Marines flushing North Korean soldiers from their bunker on Wolmi-Do Island off Inchon harbour. A total of 108 enemy were killed and 136 captured.

Captured North Korean troops on Wolmi-do island are stripped of their clothing to ensure that they do not have concealed weapons before being taken into captivity.

Marines mopping up at Wolmi-Do Island, held by 400 North Korean soldiers from the 3rd Battalion, 226th Independent Marine Regiment.

Severely wounded North Korean soldiers awaiting evacuation in September 1950.

A warehouse burns at Inchon as the Marines take a break and prepare to push on to Seoul.

A wounded Marine from I Company, 5th Marine Regiment is brought in for treatment during the fighting on the outskirts of Seoul.

Marines from the 1st Marine Division entering Seoul accompanied by late-production M4A3 (HVSS) 105mm-armed Sherman tanks, the nearest of which mounts a bulldozer blade.

Much of Seoul was destroyed as the US Marines fought their way through the streets. The Marine in the centre is armed with an M1918A2 Browning Automatic Rifle.

American troops and M4A3 (HVSS) 105mm Sherman tanks fighting their way through Seoul.

US M26 tanks lead the way into Seoul as the city changes hands for the second time. Around 20,000 North Korean troops had to be driven out first.

Marines fighting their way past a roadblock in Seoul. Note the pictures of Stalin and Kim Il Sung on the building in the background. Two of the Marines in this photograph are carrying fighting knives strapped to their boots.

Marines exchanging fire with snipers in Seoul.

A Marine marksman uses his Springfield rifle on enemy snipers in Seoul.

A Marine is about to throw a hand grenade into a tunnel to flush out North Korean soldiers in the fighting for Seoul.

A Marine taking aim during the clearing of the barricades in Seoul. Note the grenade hanging on the tunic of the bearded Corporal. The fighting in and around Seoul would continue for several days.

Mopping up was still going on in Seoul in the first week of October. The 7th US Infantry Division followed the Marines and some of them are taking cover as a Sherman tank drives over one of the North Korean barricades.

North Korean prisoners and suspect civilians are rounded up as Marines and M26 tanks advance through Seoul.

Marines with captured North Korean soldiers dressed in civilian clothes, after the recapture of Seoul.

Engineers of the 2nd Platoon, 'B' Company, 10th Engineer Combat Battalion inspect a disabled M4 Sherman tank for booby traps.

Engineers from the 2nd Engineer Combat Battalion sweep a road for anti-tank mines.

An engineer from the 16th Reconnaissance Company of the 1st Cavalry Division sets the charges on a daisy chain of explosives to detonate mines hidden in the road.

A Marine forward air-observer team guides a Marine Corsair in for a strike on an enemy-held hill. The 'Black Sheep Corsairs' were highly praised by Army and Marines alike for their precision strikes on targets and their extremely close support of forward units. The close air support provided to the 1st Marine Division by their own aircraft was unique and envied by their Army counterparts.

US Marines captured many North Korean soldiers who were little more than kids press ganged into fighting for the communists. Captured South Korean soldiers were also given the choice of changing sides or being shot on the spot.

A 0.30-calibre machine gun crew from the 5th Regimental Combat Team, 1st Cavalry Division engages targets near Taejon on 22 September 1950.

Long line of jeeps waiting to cross the river in September 1950.

Eight miles north-west of Taegu, two and a half ton trucks cross the river by an underwater bridge.

A fixed trestle bridge, part of an M4A2 bridge built by the 10th Engineer Combat Battalion.

Taejon city was virtually destroyed in the fighting to liberate it from the North Koreans in September 1950. Such scenes were responsible for the tens of thousands of refugees on the roads.

Some 400 South Korean civilians were murdered by the North Koreans in the grounds of Taejon prison before they evacuated the city. They were discovered by the US 24th Infantry Division when they recaptured the town on 28 September 1950.

These American prisoners of war were executed by the North Koreans at Taejon city jail as the UN forces closed in on the city.

An M20 75mm recoilless rifle sends another shell towards enemy lines. It was seldom effective against North Korean tanks as its high explosive projectile had little armour penetrating power.

Engineers use a rope to move a booby trapped tree from a road in the Techen-ni area in South Korea.

Officers from the 3rd ROK Division and their American advisors celebrate the crossing of the 38th Parallel into enemy territory.

Captured North Korean troops awaiting the issue of clothing and processing into a prisoner of war camp in October 1950.

This propaganda photograph shows American prisoners of war forced to carry peace banners and slogans through a North Korean town. Refusal to do so was not an option.

Air Force C-119s dropping the 187th Regimental Combat Team behind the North Korean line of retreat. They were trying to rescue hundreds of American prisoners of war being carried north by train. They would arrive too late, to discover most of the men murdered by their North Korean guards.

General MacArthur was taking a great gamble ordering his men to advance right up to the Yalu River and the border with China. The Chinese gave clear warning through diplomatic channels that they would not stand idly by and moved hundreds of thousands of troops up to the border region.

Paratroops and 1st Cavalry Division tankers meet at Sukchon, North Korea in October 1950. The tank is an M24 Chaffee, a lighter reconnaissance tank unable to stand up to the heavier T-34 in frontal engagements.

1st Cavalry Division troopers fighting their way into the North Korean capital P'yongyang.

British and Australian troops house clearing in Hwangju on 17 October 1950 on the drive towards the North Korean capital P'yongyang.

This North Korean T-34 was destroyed by the Air Force south of Suwon as it was crossing a bridge on 17 October.

Corpsmen carrying a casualty evacuated by a Marine helicopter from VMO-6 in October 1950.

Chapter Two

The Chinese Cross the Yalu

25 October – 24 December 1950

It should have come as no surprise to General MacArthur that the Chinese decided to cross the border in order to protect their interests. They certainly did not want a unified South Korea, backed by the United States, across the Yalu River. They made it clear through diplomatic channels that they would intervene if non-South Korean troops crossed the 38th Parallel.

It was not going to be easy. On 2 October Chairman Mao sent a cable to Stalin outlining the problems that they would be facing. An American Corps comprised two infantry divisions and a mechanized division with 1,500 guns of 70mm to 240mm calibre, including tank guns and anti-aircraft guns. In comparison each Chinese Army, comprising three divisions, had only thirty-six such guns. The UN dominated the air, whereas the Chinese had only just started training pilots and would not be able to deploy more than 300 aircraft in combat until February 1951. To ensure the elimination of one US Corps, the Chinese would need to assemble four times as many troops as the enemy – four field armies to deal with one enemy Corps and requiring 2,200 to 3,000 guns of more than 70mm calibre to deal with 1,500 enemy guns of the same calibre.

On 5 October 1950, the day after American troops crossed the 38th Parallel, Chairman Mao Zedong issued orders for the North East Frontier Force of the Chinese Peoples Liberation Army to move up to the Yalu River. Premier Zhou Enlai was sent to Moscow to persuade Stalin to provide aid and it was agreed that Russian Mig-15 fighters would be sent to airfields in China and painted in Chinese Air Force markings, but flown by Soviet pilots. They would not provide air-ground support to the Chinese forces, but would engage United Nations aircraft south of the Yalu River.

Because of this short delay, Mao postponed the intervention of Chinese troops from 13 October to 19 October. Four Armies and three artillery divisions were mobilized. Many were experienced troops who had fought the Japanese in the Second World War and defeated the Nationalist Army of Chiang Kai Shek afterwards. In the meantime, on the 15th President Truman flew to Wake Island to meet with General MacArthur. They discussed the possibility of Chinese intervention and Truman's desire to limit the scope of the war. MacArthur reassured Truman that the Chinese would not intervene and if they did they would be easily defeated.

On 19 October, United Nations forces entered the North Korean capital P'yongyang and on the same day the first troops from the Chinese 'Peoples Volunteer Army' crossed the Yalu River under great secrecy. As the UN forces fought their way across the North Korean countryside, General Peng Dehuai deployed his 270,000 troops in the mountains and waited for the enemy to fall into the trap.

As the South Korean troops moved into the valleys heading for the Yalu River, the Chinese watched and on 25 October, made their move. The Chinese First Phase Campaign began on the morning of 25 October when the 118th Division of the 40th Army wiped out an infantry battalion of the ROK 6th Division a mere dozen miles from the Yalu River. At the same time the 1st ROK Division ran into the Chinese 39th Army, which was tasked with the capture of Unsan. The 15th Regiment was leading the division and it ground to a halt under enemy mortar fire. Soon reports came in from the 12th Regiment on the left and the 11th Regiment in the rear – the Chinese were trying to surround the division. Colonel Paik immediately withdrew his division to Unsan and established a defensive perimeter around the town. A captured Chinese soldier was brought into his headquarters. He was wearing a thick, quilted uniform that was khaki on the outside and white on the inside and it could be worn inside out, to facilitate camouflage in snowy terrain. He admitted that he was from China's Kwangtung Province and a member of the 39th Army, sub-ordinate to the 13th Army Group. They had boarded trains in September and headed for Manchuria. They had crossed the Yalu River into Korea in mid-October, moving only at night and had gone to great efforts to conceal signs of their move-ment. He said that tens of thousands of his comrades were in the mountains around the 1st ROK Division.

The report was passed on to General Willoughby, MacArthur's chief of intel-ligence, but it was ignored. He considered that the South Koreans had encountered Chinese volunteers fighting with the North Koreans or Korean residents in China having returned to fight for their homeland. The 1st Cavalry Division was ordered to bypass the 1st ROK Division and continue the advance.

After six days of fighting the Chinese, surviving only due to US tank and artillery support the 1st ROK Division was ready to break apart. The three ROK divisions on its right flank had already retreated and Colonel Paik knew that time was running out. He recommended to General Milburn the Corps Commander, that they withdraw to the Chongchon River. They had lost over 500 men, killed or missing in action. Milburn agreed and they began to pull out as the US 8th Cavalry Regiment of the 1st Cavalry Division moved past them to cover the withdrawal.

Late in the evening of 1 November, with rocket artillery support, four Chinese battalions from their 116th Division launched their attack on two battalions of the 8th Cavalry. The sound of bugles echoed from the surrounding hills and thousands of Chinese infantry began pouring down the slopes towards the surprised cavalrymen. Throughout the night the Chinese continued their attack, overrunning one position after another. Soon they were so close that the artillery fire was no longer effective and the two battalions tried to withdraw. However, by now the Chinese had got behind them and established roadblocks on the main routes out of the town. The infantrymen split up into small groups and took to the hills to try to find their way to safety.

Early in the morning of 2 November the human wave of Chinese fell upon the 3rd Battalion of the 8th Cavalry. They helped to seal their own fate by allowing a company of Chinese commandos dressed in South Korean uniforms to cross a bridge near the battalion command post, thinking that they were ROK troops. Once across the bridge, the Chinese commander blew his bugle and, throwing satchel charges and grenades, his men overran the command post and killed many men still in their sleeping bags.

The 5th Cavalry Regiment tried to break through the Chinese encircling the 8th Cavalry, but they were unable to cut their way through the determined enemy and after suffering 350 casualties they withdrew, leaving the survivors of the 8th Cavalry to fight their way to safety. Over 800 of them did not make it, either dying on the battlefield or surrendering to the victorious Chinese. It was the most devastating loss to the US forces so far in the war.

2 November was the day that the UN Offensive Campaign came to a halt. The US-named Chinese Communist Forces Intervention Campaign began the next day, 3 November and it would last until 24 January the following year. The destruction of the 8th Cavalry heralded a change in the balance of power and it began to shift in favour of the communists. They would refer to those fateful eleven days, 25 October to 5 November as their Chinese First Offensive.

Other elements of the Eighth Army were also attacked and by 6 November the UN forces had pulled back to the line of the Chongchon River, which runs from the west coast in a north-easterly direction towards the Chosin Reservoir. Then as suddenly as they had appeared, the Chinese vanished into the hills and valleys of the land stretching towards the border with China.

The Chinese had intended to push the UN forces back across the Chongchon River and into P'yongyang, but they were running short of food and ammunition and were forced to disengage on 5 November, thus ending the Chinese First Phase Campaign. Apart from their victory at Unsan, they had also destroyed the ROK 6th Infantry Division and one regiment from the 8th Division at the battle of Onjong. In return, they had suffered nearly 11,000 casualties.

The Chinese victory at Unsan was a surprise to the Chinese leadership and they intensely studied the performance of the 1st Cavalry Division. It was noted that the American mechanized forces moved fast and established defence works quickly. It was unfavourable to assault such defences with massed infantry attacks.

General MacArthur could have halted the march to the Yalu River after the heavy losses suffered by the Eighth Army at Unsan. It was clear that the Chinese intended to defend the power stations supplying electricity to Manchuria and that to continue advancing was to run the risk of full scale war with China. He was undeterred and launched a 'Home by Christmas' offensive. Historians still debate whether he had convinced himself that only a weak Chinese force was present in Korea, or whether he wanted to deliberately provoke war with China.

General Peng suggested to Mao that the UN forces might be lured into preset ambushes as far north as possible, stretching their supply lines and isolating them from each other. Mao approved the plan and Peng instructed each CPVF Army to withdraw its main force further north, but leave one division to lure the UN forces into the trap. They even released some 100 prisoners of war, including twenty-seven Americans, who were deliberately told that they were being released because the Volunteers had to return to China due to supply difficulties.

At this time the US-led United Nations Command comprised the Eighth Army headquarters and the ROK Army headquarters, three US and three ROK Corps headquarters, eighteen infantry divisions – ten ROK and seven US Army and one US Marine, three Allied brigades and a separate airborne regiment. Total ground forces came to 425,000 men, including 178,000 Americans, plus major air and navy elements including aircraft carriers and fighters and bombers based in South Korea and Japan.

Opposing them were the North Korean Army of eight Corps and thirty divisions plus several brigades, although only two Corps of five weakened divisions and two brigades were actually engaged in combat with UN forces. The remainder of their forces had either withdrawn across the Yalu River into Manchuria or were avoiding combat in the mountains along the border. The main combat unit opposing the UN advance was the 300,000 strong Chinese Peoples Volunteer Army. The hilly terrain on the northern bank of the Chongchon River formed a defensive barrier that allowed the Chinese to hide their presence, while the UN forces advanced. To make things worse, the battle was also fought over one of the coldest winters in 100 years, with temperatures falling as low as $-30°F$ ($-34°C$).

With the disappearance of the Chinese forces, the UN advance resumed on 24 November with General Walker's Eighth Army moving up the west coast and General Almond's X Corps due to start moving up the east coast three days later. The two forces were separated by the virtually impassable Taebaek Mountains. The Eighth Army comprised the reconstituted ROK II Corps on the right flank and leading the advance the US I Corps to the west with the US IX Corps in the centre. They moved cautiously in line to prevent a repeat of the earlier ambushes in the first Chinese campaign. Despite their lack of manpower, the US Eighth Army had three and a half times the firepower of the opposing Chinese forces. In addition the US Fifth Air Force providing the air support, had little opposition due to the lack of Chinese anti-aircraft weapons.

Morale among the American troops was high, boosted by a Thanksgiving feast with roast turkey on the eve of the advance. However, this led to overconfidence and some of the men had discarded equipment and ammunition before the advance. One rifle company from the US IX Corps began its advance without carrying helmets or bayonets and there were less on average than one grenade and fifty rounds of ammunition carried per man. In addition, because the US planners did not foresee that the campaign would continue into the winter, the men of Eighth Army started the advance with a shortage of winter clothing.

What they did not know was that the 13th Peoples Volunteer Army Group was hiding in the mountains, with the 50th and 66th Army to the west, the 39th and 40th Army in the centre and the 38th and 42nd Army in the east. General Peng's plan was for the 38th and 42nd Army to first attack the ROK II Corps and destroy the UN right flank, then cut behind the UN lines. At the same time the 39th and 40th Army would hold the US IX Corps in place, so it could not reinforce the ROK II Corps. The 50th and 66th Army would check the advance of the US I Corps.

A Chinese Army was similar to a Corps in the American Army, consisting of three divisions of around 10,000 men each, although actual strength was usually 7,000– 8,500. Each division had three 3,000-man regiments of infantry, whereas an American division consisted of three regiments of infantry, three battalions of 105mm artillery, one battalion of 155mm artillery, an anti-aircraft battalion, a tank battalion and other supporting units, totalling 20,000 men.

The Chinese forces were basically infantrymen, with almost no heavy weapons other than mortars. There was also only one rifle available for every three Chinese, mostly captured from Japanese during the Second World War or the Chinese Nationalist forces during the civil war. Most were US made small arms such as the Thompson sub-machine gun, M1 Garand Rifle, M1918 Browning Automatic Rifle, the bazooka and the M2 mortar. They were encouraged to use captured enemy weapons whenever possible and to take weapons from their dead comrades. Because most of their artillery had been left behind in Manchuria, mortars were the only heavy support available for the Chinese. For the coming offensive the average soldier was issued with five days' worth of rations and ammunition. To compensate for these shortcomings, the Chinese relied extensively on night attacks and infiltration to avoid the UN firepower. As they had little mechanized transport they could avoid the roads and manoeuvre over the hills, bypassing the UN defences and surrounding isolated UN positions.

Four of the Chinese armies, the 38th, 40th, 50th and 66th, struck the Eighth Army, on the night of 25 November. The 40th Army hit the three regiments of the US 2nd Infantry Division at Kunu-ri on the Chongchon River, as well as the US 25th Infantry Division on their left flank. Although they suffered heavy casualties, the Chinese pressed on with their attack, tying down the American units while a new offensive fell on the ROK II Corps on the right hand side of the Eighth Army line. The 38th Army broke through the ROK line in the gap between the 7th and 8th Divisions and established roadblocks to their rear and by the end of 26 November the II ROK Corps front broke and the South Koreans began to retreat, thus exposing the right flank of the Eighth Army.

Heavy attacks on the US 25th Infantry Division and the ROK 1st Division soon followed and both units began to retreat under the pressure. The village of Kunu-ri became a major bottleneck for the US IX Corps' retreat and in an effort to stabilize the front on 28 November, General Walker ordered the US 2nd Infantry Division to withdraw and set up a new defensive line at Kunu-ri. General Peng had also recognized the importance of the village and ordered his 38th Army to cut the IX Corps line of retreat. Its 114th Division was to capture Kunu-ri while the 112th Division would follow on a parallel route through the hills north of the road.

By mid-afternoon on 28 November all US and ROK forces were in retreat. The retreat was made even more difficult by the thousands of refugees heading south away from the fighting. Amongst them were North Korean and Chinese infiltrators, dressed in civilian clothes, who would pass the American check points and then turn and open fire on them. Eventually the ROK Police would try to route the columns of refugees away from the roads, while on other occasions both US and ROK troops would open fire on refugees coming near to their positions.

The US 2nd Infantry Division was positioned in the centre of Eighth Army's front, with the Turkish Brigade ten miles away on its right flank. The Turkish Brigade was ordered to block the Chinese advance and suffered heavy casualties before it broke out and joined up with the 2nd Division on 29 November. This delaying action allowed the 2nd Division to secure Kunu-ri on the night of 28 November.

On the night of 28 November General MacArthur gathered his field commanders for a conference in Tokyo. He instructed Walker to withdraw from the battle before the Chinese could surround the Eighth Army and retreat to a new line at Sunchon, thirty miles south of Kunu-ri.

The full weight of the Chinese offensive now fell on Lieutenant General Laurence B. Keiser's 2nd Infantry Division as it prepared to withdraw from Kunu-ri. The Chinese 113th Division had advanced forty-five miles in fourteen hours and now occupied strategic points in the rear of the Division where they established road blocks on the division's withdrawal route south to Sunchon.

General Keiser believed that the Chinese only had one roadblock four miles from his position, but in fact they had constructed a series of reinforced roadblocks throughout the length of the entire valley. As the division began to withdraw on the morning of 30 November, it found itself having to 'run the gauntlet' of the road blocks and the thousands of Chinese occupying the high ground along the route. By the time the General realized his mistake, it was too late to turn the division around and take the road to the east and then south to Sinanju. The main Chinese advance was being held back by the 23rd Infantry Regiment, commanded by Colonel Freeman and he did not feel that they could hold out long enough for the entire division to turn around and return to the Sinanju road. The division would just have to run the gauntlet.

At 1300 hours a column of US tanks led the way through the valley. They came under intense fire and had to stop twice to push aside barricades of destroyed Turkish trucks set up by the Chinese. By 1400 hours they were clear of the ambush and had linked up with British troops from the 29th Commonwealth Brigade sent to clear the road to the south. Unfortunately, while the tankers had to stop to clear the barricades, the trucks following them also had to halt. Then the soft-skinned vehicles became easy targets for the Chinese machine guns and mortars. Their occupants would have to exit the vehicles and take cover in the ditches at the side of the road and watch their trucks being destroyed. When there was a lull in the firing, drivers would scramble out of the ditches and back into their trucks and drive on, without waiting for their passengers to climb back on board.

Lieutenant Colonel William Kelleher of the 1st Battalion, 38th Infantry Regiment later recalled: 'For the next 500 yards the road was temporarily impassable because of the numerous burning vehicles and the pile up of the dead men, coupled with the rush of the wounded from the ditches, struggling to get aboard anything that rolled … either there would be bodies in our way, or we would be almost borne down by wounded men who literally threw themselves upon us … I squeezed a wounded ROK soldier into our trailer, but as I put him aboard, other wounded men piled on the trailer in such numbers that the jeep couldn't pull ahead. It was necessary to beat them off.'

The most dangerous part of the road leading south to Sunchon was an area known simply as 'The Pass' where the hillside was steepest and the road was at its most narrow point. Most of the casualties occurred in this bottleneck. Soon the road was littered with dead and dying troops and by the time General Yazici's Turkish brigade came to take its turn, all road movement had stopped because of the number of destroyed and abandoned trucks on the road. Two companies of Turks fixed bayonets and charged up the eastern slope of the mountains, while US air support strafed the Chinese positions. General Keiser sent two of his remaining tanks to clear the wreckage on the route and the following columns began to creep forward again.

In the meantime, Colonel Freeman realized what was happening in the valley to his rear and very wisely decided to take his men down the road to the east. In one of the last acts of the battle, the 23rd Infantry Regiment fired off its stock of 3,206 artillery shells within twenty minutes and the massive barrage shocked the Chinese troops from following the regiment. They broke contact with the Chinese and the 23rd Infantry Regiment lived to fight another day. The other units of 2nd Division would not be so lucky. As night fell, General Keiser lost his air support and the Chinese infantry crawled down the hillsides to swarm over the road. The brunt of their attack fell on the 38th and 503rd Field Artillery Battalions and the 2nd Engineer Combat Battalion, who had to abandon their equipment and fight their way out on foot. The majority of them would be killed or captured.

The commander of the 2nd Engineer Battalion, Colonel Alarich Zacherle, had asked General Keiser days before the start of the Chinese offensive, to redeploy his unit south to P'yongyang, as their bridging equipment and bulldozers would not be needed in the mountains. He refused and only 266 of the 900 men of the battalion survived. The Colonel would spend the rest of the war in a Chinese prison camp.

With the road now blocked with the destroyed equipment of the two artillery battalions, the rest of the division was forced to take to the hills and find a way past the hordes of Chinese. The US 2nd Infantry Division had ceased to exist as an effective fighting force; it was the greatest US defeat of the whole war.

Most of the division's transport was lost during the retreat; the 37th Field Artillery Battalion for example, lost thirty-five men, ten howitzers, fifty-three vehicles and thirty-nine trailers. Unit integrity broke down and there were recriminations afterwards when it became clear that the divisional commander and other ranking officers had escaped, leaving 4,500 men, almost a third of the division's strength dead or in captivity. At that time, a US infantry regiment was authorized 3,800 men and from the three regiments in the division, the 9th Infantry lost 1,474 men, the 38th Infantry lost 1,178 men and the 23rd Infantry 545 men. The division also lost sixty-four artillery pieces, hundreds of trucks and nearly all of its engineer equipment. The Chinese and North Koreans would make good use of their war booty over the coming months, while columns of weary 2nd Division prisoners of war trudged their way north to communist prison camps. It was estimated that 3,000 US POWs were taken, the largest such group captured by the Chinese during the war.

The other US unit to report significant losses was the US 25th Infantry Division with 1,313 casualties. The Turkish Brigade was rendered ineffective after losing 936 casualties, along with 90 per cent of its equipment and vehicles and 50 per cent of its artillery. Chinese casualties were estimated at 45,000 with half due to combat and the rest to the lack of adequate winter clothing and the lack of food. For its role in establishing the Gauntlet against the US 2nd Infantry Division the Chinese 38th Army was awarded the title 'Ten Thousand Years Army' by General Peng on 1 December 1950.

The Eighth Army was now reduced to two Corps, composed of four divisions and two brigades, so General Walker ordered his Army to abandon North Korea on 3 December, much to the surprise of the Chinese commanders. The following 120 mile withdrawal to the 38th Parallel is often referred to as the longest retreat in US military history. Walker was unaware that the Chinese 13th Army Group was half-starved and incapable of further offensive operations. The great 'Bug Out' had begun.

Across the other side of the peninsula, General Almond's X Corps had begun moving northwards on 27 November, with the two divisions of the ROK I Corps following the coastal roads, the US 7th Infantry Division in the centre and the 1st Marine Division on the left, all aiming for different points on the Yalu River. The Marines were to pass along both sides of the Chosin Reservoir, tie in with the right flank of Eighth Army and then press on a further sixty miles to the Yalu. The commander of the 1st Marine Division, Major General Oliver P. Smith, was wary of advancing too fast, despite the insistence of the Corps commander. The terrain in that part of Korea consisted of narrow roads, often cut by gullies and valleys with imposing ridgelines and mountains surrounding them. Smith wanted his men to advance cautiously, in contact with each other and maintaining unit integrity. He made the correct decision.

General Almond then ordered the 31st Regimental Combat Team of the 7th Division to relieve the 5th Marine Regiment on the east side of the Chosin Reservoir, so the Marines could concentrate their forces in the west. However, the 31st RCT as well as the rest of the 7th Division were widely scattered and the units arrived at the east of the reservoir in bits and pieces. They eventually formed themselves into Task Force Faith and Task Force McLean, named after their commanders.

Late on 27 November, the Chinese Offensive began on the eastern front with the 150,000 strong Ninth Army Group, comprising the 20th, 26th and 27th Armies advancing towards the 1st Marine Division and the US 7th Infantry Division. The CPVF 79th and 89th Divisions fell on the 5th and 7th Marine Regiments on the west side of the reservoir and the 80th Division surrounded Task Force McLean on the east side. During heavy fighting Colonel McLean was captured and Colonel Faith took over command. The 2,500 men of Task Force Faith tried to break through to the Marines in the south, taking their 600 wounded men with them. The Chinese were too strong for them though and only half would eventually make it through. The wounded Colonel Faith and all of the wounded were left behind to their fate.

To the west of the reservoir, the 5th and 7th Marines began a fighting withdrawal back to Hagaru-ri at the south end of the reservoir and then a further fifty miles south-east to Hungnam, a port on the east coast from where they would be withdrawn by sea. The epic retreat would see the 1st Marine Division bring their dead and wounded with them as they fought their way slowly to safety. During the day they could rely on close air support from their own aircraft, but during the night they had to contend with the bitter cold and the Chinese creeping closer and closer to their columns. Finally, 11,000 Marines and 1,000 Infantry soldiers made it to Hungnam where they were taken off by the Navy. They were followed by the ROK I Corps, the battered US 7th Infantry Division and the newly arrived US 3rd Infantry Division: over 105,000 troops, 18,000 vehicles and 350,000 tons of bulk cargo, as well as 98,000 refugees. On 24 December the port was evacuated and all remaining stores in the warehouses ashore destroyed in a massive series of explosions. The ships were heading for Pusan in the South, where the troops would be refitted and redeployed to the front to help Eighth Army hold the line.

Although the Chinese Ninth Army Group scored the CPVF's only major victory in three years of war when it wiped out the entire 32nd Regiment of the 7th Division, it suffered terribly in the Korean winter. More than 30,000 officers and men, some 22 per cent of the entire Army Group, were disabled by severe frostbite and over a thousand died.

In the meantime Eighth Army had pulled back from the Chongchon River and was concentrating near P'yongyang. General Walker realized that his forces were in no condition to hold a defensive line so far north and approved a further withdrawal of almost a hundred miles to the Imjin River, north of Seoul. By the end of December the UN line was established with the US I and IX Corps and the ROK III, II and I Corps running from the west coast to east. The Chinese did not pursue them; they needed to resupply and refit, as did the UN forces now licking their wounds and digging new defensive positions along the Imjin River. The Second Campaign represented the peak of CPVF performance in the Korean War. From now on things would get harder. They were hampered by their weak firepower compared to the UN forces and they would have to follow them southwards to continue the battle, where the enemy's superior weapons and air power could be brought to bear on them. There were logistical constraints as well; an overstretched supply line, bad roads, a shortage of trucks and marauding UN aircraft combined to cause food shortages where some CPVF units only had food for one week.

General Walker's part in the war came to an end on the morning of 23 December, while he was out on an inspection tour in his jeep. Ten miles north of Seoul, a Korean truck driver pulled onto the wrong side of the road and collided head on with his jeep, killing the General. He would be replaced by Lieutenant General Matthew B. Ridgway, a famed airborne commander from the Second World War, whose first task would be to turn morale around and improve the fighting ability of the Eighth Army.

A machine gun crew from the US 2nd Infantry Division north of the Chongchon River on 20 November 1950.

British Royal Marines from 41 Commando, put ashore by a US naval vessel deep in the heart of North Korea, plant demolition charges along an enemy rail track. They were attached to the 1st Marine Division and fought with them at the Chosin Reservoir.

Marine Corsairs drop napalm on North Korean positions on the drive towards the Chosin reservoir.

Chinese General Peng Dehuai left, confers with North Korean leader Kim Il Sung.

14 October 1950, the 334th Regiment, 119th Division, 15th Chinese Field Army cross the frozen Yalu River into North Korea. The first units took up positions near the power generating stations that supplied electricity to most of Manchuria.

Chinese troops hiding in a bunker in a hillside. They managed to keep the presence of thirty-eight Divisions totalling 300,000 men, hidden from UN eyes until they launched their First Phase Offensive on 25 October 1950.

Chinese communist infantry moving to an attack through the snow. Their rubber-soled canvas shoes provided no protection against the cold and frostbite caused more casualties than UN firepower in the winter of 1950.

The Peoples Liberation Army's communications were inferior in comparison to the UN forces. Radios were only issued down to regiments, who then used field telephones if available, to contact their battalions. Battalions then used bugles, whistles and runners to talk to each other and their subordinate companies.

The Chinese 40th Corps attack American positions near the Chosin Reservoir. A Chinese Corps was the equivalent to an American division.

Captain Warren J. Rosengren interrogates a captured Chinese soldier near Kunang in North Korea. South Korean military policemen stand guard while an interpreter translates.

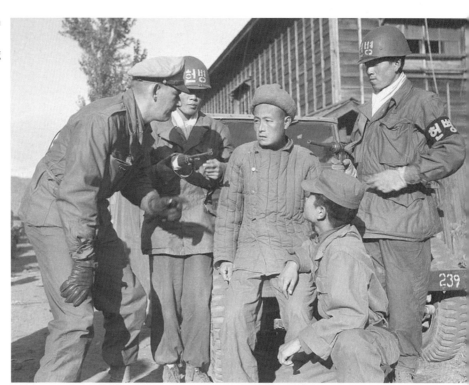

Early reports of dead Chinese soldiers were initially ignored. It was not until live prisoners were interrogated that the awful truth dawned — China had joined the conflict.

Troopers from the 8th Cavalry Regiment advancing cautiously into North Korea. The unit would be decimated near Unsan in October when it was overrun by human waves of Chinese infantry.

Corporal Sam Ayala, L Company, 7th Regimental Combat Team, US 3rd Infantry Division nurses his wounds as his comrades take a break from the fighting.

Chinese troops prepare to assault the US 31st Regimental Combat Team. Known as Task Force Faith after its commander, the unit was destroyed between 27 November and 2 December 1950 whilst guarding the right flank of the 1st Marine Division as it withdrew from the Chosin Reservoir.

Chinese troops pour from their hiding places to encircle the 1st Marine Division as it reached the Chosin Reservoir. The US 7th Infantry Division suffered heavy casualties at the northern end of the reservoir.

Chinese troops take a break to drink tea.

Chinese reinforcements advancing into North Korea. The Chinese enjoyed a virtually unlimited supply of manpower. Note the foliage being carried by the soldiers; the concealment skills of the Chinese were legendary.

Refugees fleeing P'yongyang cross the Taedong River on 4 December 1950 on the ruins of this road bridge.

An anti-tank mine crew search the ground after an M4A3E8 76 W (HVSS) Sherman tank from the 32nd Regimental Combat Team, US 7th Infantry Division was disabled when it hit a mine on the road.

A North Korean flag captured in the Chosin Reservoir area.

Chinese troops firing mortar rounds at a UN hilltop position while the infantry advances.

This sixteen-foot hole was blown by Chinese soldiers in the single road from the Chosin Reservoir to the sea. Bridge sections were dropped by C-119s to span the gap and allow the retreat to continue.

Chinese prisoners taken by 'C' Company, 7th Marines south of Koto-ri on 9 December 1950 during the retreat from the Chosin Reservoir.

Marines in the retreat from the Chosin Reservoir halt while leading elements clear a Chinese roadblock.

These Marines can still raise a smile for the camera despite the atrocious weather conditions. A light 60mm mortar with its base plate lies on the ground in the snow.

Casualties being loaded onto a USAF C-47 at the tiny Hagaru-ri airstrip during the retreat from the Chosin Reservoir. A total of 4,312 casualties were evacuated in five days.

Frozen bodies of American Marines, British Commandos and South Korean soldiers are gathered for a group burial at Koto-ri.

Men of the 5th Marine Regiment receive medals at Hungnam prior to their withdrawal by sea.

No photographs have been found of the US 2nd Infantry Division running the gauntlet at Kunu-ri in November 1950 but there would have been similar scenes to this, with men sheltering in ditches and behind vehicles as the Chinese poured fire down on them from the hills above.

A Chinese photograph showing American officers and soldiers who were captured in the destruction of the US 2nd Infantry Division near Kunu-ri. The Division suffered almost 5,000 casualties, a third of its strength and almost all of its artillery and engineer equipment.

At the port of Hungnam the remaining fuel, ammunitions and supplies are destroyed on 24 December 1950 as USS *Begor* stands off in the harbour.

Chapter Three

The Great Bug Out

31 December 1950 – 8 July 1951

The Second Chinese offensive had eventually petered out as they ran short of supplies. The units on the western front had fewer than 300 trucks to carry supplies for 300,000 troops and the Ninth Army Group was disabled due to frostbite. General Peng requested a pause of a few months until the spring and wanted to confine his forthcoming campaign to areas north of the 38th Parallel. The UN had proposed a cease-fire to the Chinese on 1 December, which Mao interpreted as a weakness that China should exploit. Mao overruled Peng and ordered him to plan a third campaign across the 38th Parallel against UN forces entrenched across the entire peninsula. It would stretch the fragile Chinese supply lines to breaking point and allow Eighth Army to inflict severe losses on them in the spring of 1951.

The Chinese soldiers subsisted on *Shaoping*, a hard, unleavened bread. Each man carried his own measure of a concoction of sorghum, millet, lima beans and wheat flour from which he prepared the bread, eating while on the move. The Chinese soldiers had little opportunity to enjoy hot food because the UN air superiority and continual air reconnaissance prevented them from building fires. This unvaried diet of cold food caused large numbers of Chinese soldiers to suffer diseases of the digestive tract.

The South Korean soldiers lived off a basic dish of steamed rice, often mixed with barley and supplemented with salted fish and soybean and red pepper paste. They ate very little meat, but made soup from boiled vegetables or bean sprouts. With the virtual absence of communist aircraft over the battlefield, the ROK troops had no trouble building fires to cook their meals.

The American soldiers consumed three grades of rations: A, B and C. The A rations were top quality western food including steak; B rations were simpler foods like sausage, that could be heated and eaten by an individual or prepared for a unit. The famous C rations were field rations, canned and easily carried in the field.

As of January 1951 the Eighth Army consisted of 178,000 American soldiers and Marines, 224,000 ROK Army troops and contingents from the United Kingdom,

Australia, Canada, Turkey and many other countries. They were organized into five corps, from west to east: I Corps, IX Corps and X Corps and the ROK III and I Corps. Generally, the ROK units held the more easily defended, rugged terrain in the east, while the US forces were positioned on the lower, flatter areas in the west, where their greater firepower and mobility were more decisive.

Opposing the UN forces were some 290,000 Chinese and North Korean soldiers. The Chinese were organized into seven Corps-sized armies and twenty-two divisions totalling 204,000 troops, primarily holding the western and central portions of the front. Around 50,000 North Korean soldiers in three Corps and fourteen under-strength divisions, held the eastern sector. In addition, a further 30,000 North Korean guerillas were still behind the UN lines in the mountainous areas of eastern South Korea.

The Chinese method of attacking eventually became clear to the UN Command. They would aim for the juncture of two UN forces, where it was difficult for one to support the other by fire, or for a point where the defences were not very deep. Before the communist troops moved on foot to the attack point, they were issued with five to seven days' combat rations and were warned not to eat them until needed. Basic loads of ammunition were also issued and the troops were told to use captured UN material whenever possible. At this assembly area the battalion commanders were given their zones of attack. Their men would advance in columns of battalions to the attack point at about 2,500 yards per hour. About 2,000 metres from the enemy front lines the communist troops would be given a short rest and allowed to eat one combat ration. At this point, company commanders were given their orders and took over from the battalion commanders. The method of attack and the time element would be controlled by the divisional commander. No flexibility was permitted to the battalion and company commanders. When the order to attack was given, the company and platoon commanders would give their orders by whistle or bugle and the infantry would close with the enemy as quickly as possible to avoid the defensive artillery fire and overwhelm them with superior numbers.

On New Years Eve 1950 the CPVF launched its Third Campaign and in a matter of eight days had crossed the 38th Parallel, recaptured Seoul without a fight and pushed the UN forces back to the 37th Parallel. The UN forces destroyed or abandoned huge supply dumps as they retreated, to be pillaged by passing friendly troops or the advancing Chinese. American sleeping bags were favoured by the Chinese, who suffered more casualties as a result of the extreme weather than American guns.

On the morning of 3 January 1951, it was the turn of the British 29th Independent Infantry Brigade to face the Chinese as they swarmed southwards. They were near Koyang, twelve miles north-west of Seoul. The snow lay thick on the ground and a bitter wind howled in from Manchuria as they took up their positions, to the right of the US 35th Infantry Regiment. The Americans were the first to engage the Chinese as they advanced blowing whistles and bugles, then they fell upon the Irishmen of the 1st Royal Ulster Rifles. Two platoons were overrun and acting battalion commander Major Tony Blake called in artillery and air support before a counter-attack was launched and hand-to-hand fighting with bayonets, hand grenades, sten guns, boots and fists spread across the hill. As dawn approached the Chinese withdrew, leaving 300 dead behind them. By the time the order to withdraw reached the Ulstermen, they would be the last UN unit to withdraw; the American infantry had already pulled out and the hills were swarming with Chinese.

Their line of retreat would lead them down a valley overlooked by the Chinese. The retreat began on a frozen, moonless night and the columns of soldiers, their vehicles in the centre, moved stealthily down the steel-hard track. An armoured force of a dozen Cromwell tanks from Cooper Force was following them, their tracks squealing and slipping on the ice. Suddenly, just as the leading company met up with the waiting American trucks at the valley mouth, an American plane appeared over-head and dropped flares into the valley. The column was bathed in an eerie white light as the Irishmen swore under their breaths. The enemy could not fail to spot them and opened up with their mortars and machine guns. Then hundreds of Chinese poured down the hills to seize a village on the southern track, blocking the route.

Major John Shaw, the Support Company commander led a charge through the blazing village and into the hills. In the meantime the Cromwell tanks tried to clear the six mile long icy track that the infantry had to negotiate to join the main highway. They were unsuccessful; some of the tanks ran off the road and became stuck and others were destroyed by the Chinese infantry. Of the sixty-five men in the tank crews, only eleven escaped the carnage in 'Happy Valley'. The rest were killed or captured. Over 150 of the Irishmen were lost during the battle, as they fought their way clear of the trap and on to the waiting US trucks for a ride across the Han River pontoon bridge to safety. They were the last unit to cross the river before the bridges were blown up behind them.

On 25 January 1951, only seventeen days after the CPVF stopped its pursuit, General Ridgway ordered the launch of Operation Thunderbolt and by 31 January the US I and IX Corps had moved up to twenty miles into the area south of Seoul. Generally opposition was light and the Chinese merely fought rearguard actions, rather than holding their ground. As January came to an end, Chinese resistance began to increase, indicating that the main enemy defensive line had almost been reached. On 27 January, the US 3rd Division joined the attack in the I Corps sector and two days later Ridgway ordered a full scale offensive with X Corps joining in on its eastern flank. I and IX Corps continued a steady advance to the Han River against heavier Chinese defences. On 9 February, the enemy line of defence opposite I and IX Corps gave way and the UN forces raced ahead. The 25th Infantry Division retook

Inchon and Kimpo airfield, while elements of I Corps reached the south bank of the Han River opposite Seoul.

With the three US Corps advancing in the west and centre of the country, Ridgway ordered the ROK III Corps to begin Operation Roundup. The ROK 5th and 8th Infantry Divisions were to retake Hongchon and destroy the North Korean forces in that area. They were supported by the US 2nd and 7th Infantry Divisions and the 187th Airborne Regimental Combat Team.

As the UN forces advanced steadily, the Chinese were preparing a counter-offensive, massing in the central sector north of Hoengsong. On the night of 11–12 February, the enemy began his Fourth Campaign with five Chinese Armies and two North Korean Corps, numbering 135,000 men. Their main effort was against the ROK divisions, particularly the 8th Division which suffered heavy losses and they retreated south-east through the snow-covered passes in the rugged mountains. They were being supported by the US 15th Field Artillery Battalion which was also overrun by the Chinese despite the best efforts of their quad-50 machine guns, although they disabled their 105mm howitzers before retreating. One of the gunners taken prisoner that day was Oscar Cortez, who recalled: 'The South Koreans were passing by in a hurry and right after I heard the Chinese bugles and our quad fifties start firing. All hell broke loose. We got our march order, hooked up our 105s and were ready to move out. It was night and we waited for daylight, but we couldn't move because we were pinned down. We finally broke out and we received machine-gun fire along the way. Bullets came close to my head but I was lucky, they didn't reach me, maybe because the truck was moving pretty fast. We stopped along the way in an open field and started firing point-blank at the swarm of oncoming Chinese. Since the ground was frozen and we couldn't dig in the trails of our 105, I had to stand on the trail itself and fire the gun. The recoil would send the gun sliding back, so I had to push the gun back into firing position and do it all over again until we ran out of ammo.'

Oscar Cortez was one of many prisoners captured by the Chinese and joined one of the columns of POWs trudging northwards. They would find little comfort in the prisoner of war camps. Around the first week of February fifty prisoners were marched out onto the frozen parade ground of Compound 105 in Camp 5 near Pyoktong. They were made to stand for four hours exposed to the extreme cold as punishment for losing two propaganda pamphlets that the Chinese had tried to force them to read. As a result many of them suffered exposure and caught pneumonia, a potentially fatal illness when you are half-starved and exhausted. It was between twenty and thirty degrees below freezing in the unheated buildings and there were never less than 350 cases of pneumonia a day in the camp. Between twenty-eight and thirty-five men died every day and the bodies of hundreds of prisoners are still buried in the hills above the camp.

As the enemy turned the right flank of the UN offensive, a general withdrawal began in the centre section and most of the recently won terrain was given up again. On 13 February, the Chinese moved against the US 2nd Infantry Division positions near Chipyong-ni on the left of the X Corps front. A key road junction, surrounded by a ring of small hills, Chipyong-ni would give the Chinese access to the nearby Han River Valley, where they would threaten the positions of the I and IX Corps west of the river. The 23rd Infantry Regiment and its attached French Battalion dug in and were soon surrounded. The Air Force supplied close air support and flew resupply missions for the beleaguered defenders. That night three Chinese divisions, supported by artillery, assaulted the two-mile perimeter. The attackers were stopped on the edge of the American positions only by extensive artillery support and automatic weapons fire from an attached anti-aircraft battalion.

To the south-east, the situation was grave as the enemy exploited the large gaps in the UN line until the 27th British Commonwealth Brigade and the ROK 6th Division moved into the gap south of Chipyong-ni. The 5th Cavalry Regiment, reinforced with field artillery and tank units eventually broke through the Chinese lines to relieve the 23rd Infantry at Chipyong-ni. Captured documents indicated that the Chinese had lost 5,000 men trying to take the area.

By 18 February, the communist offensive was spent and UN reinforcements had stabilized the line. Rather than attempting to hold the land they had won, the Chinese began withdrawing to the north, where they could resupply and replace their casualties and move away from the strong UN firepower. Ridgway decided to continue to pursue the retreating Chinese and Operation Killer began on 20 February with all five Corps slowly moving forward through the mud and rain. He hoped that the name 'Killer' would help encourage the offensive spirit of the Eighth Army, which had taken a battering over the last couple of months. By 28 February, all units had reached their objectives and had eliminated all enemy forces south of the Han River.

Operation Ripper was launched on 7 March, to continue the advance for a further twenty or thirty miles, to recapture Seoul and the towns of Hongchon, fifty miles west of Seoul and Chunchon, fifteen miles farther to the north. Ridgway's objective now was to restore South Korea's pre-war boundaries and to destroy as much of the enemy's forces as possible. The offensive was preceded by one of the largest UN artillery bombardments of the war. On the left of the UN front, the US 25th Infantry Division crossed the Han River and established a bridgehead. During the night of 14–15 March, units of the ROK 1st Division and the US 3rd Infantry Division recaptured Seoul, the capital city changing hands for the fourth and last time in the war.

Although the operation recaptured lost ground, the Chinese pulled back before they suffered too many casualties, so Operation Courageous was prepared, with the aim of trapping the Chinese and North Korean forces north of Seoul, in the area between the Han and Imjin Rivers. The 187th Airborne Regimental Combat Team would drop from 100 C-119 Boxcar aircraft onto the south bank of the Imjin River, twenty miles north of the current front line. In the meantime Task Force Growdon, made up of armoured units from the 6th Medium Tank Battalion from the US 24th Infantry Division and infantry from the US 3rd Infantry Division negotiated their way through enemy minefields to link up with the paratroopers on the 23 March. One of the main objectives of the airborne operation was to cut off and destroy some 6,000 men of the newly organized NKPA I Corps. However, the enemy had continued to retreat faster than the UN forces could advance and most of them escaped.

By the end of March, the Eighth Army units were nearing the 38th Parallel, but there were signs that the Chinese and North Koreans were preparing to launch their own spring offensive. Before it began, Ridgway, backed by General MacArthur and President Truman decided to move even further north to take over more defensible positions. Operation Rugged was planned to secure a new line, Kansas, just north of the 38th Parallel, while Operation Dauntless would extend the front line a further twenty miles northwards to line Wyoming. The new front line would be heavily defended and when the communist offensive was launched, the defenders would conduct a fighting withdrawal to Line Kansas, while causing the maximum amount of casualties to the enemy. The main defensive battle would then be fought along Line Kansas.

By 20 April, the UN forces were established along Line Kansas, but before Operation Rugged could commence, the communist forces launched their spring offensive across the entire UN front on 22 April. By now General MacArthur had been relieved by President Truman and replaced by General Matthew B. Ridgway. Lieutenant General James A. Van Fleet took over command of the US Eighth Army.

The new Chinese offensive, aimed at the recapture of Seoul, was their fifth of the war and its impact was felt along the 116 mile length of Line Kansas. Three Army Groups of almost 700,000 men were moving southwards and US I Corps was their first objective. The ROK 6th Division bore the brunt of the initial assault, west of the Hwachon Reservoir and when the enemy broke through, it exposed the flanks of the US 24th Infantry Division and the 1st Marine Division. The next day the Chinese completed the rout of the ROK division and poured through the gap, advancing twenty miles south-west of the Hwachon Reservoir. They ran into the British 27th Brigade and its attached US 72nd Tank Battalion which held them off while the UN forces withdrew. A series of intense battles were fought by US and multinational forces as the enemy crossed the Imjin River and established bridgeheads on the southern bank.

The Hwachon Reservoir and Dam was an important strategic objective for both sides. When the Chinese captured the reservoir they opened the crest spillway gates on the dam and the quantity of water released raised the level of the Han River by four feet and destroyed two UN bridges. The 4th Ranger Company of the 1st Cavalry Division was dispatched to conduct a raid on the dam and disable the gates but its efforts failed. The 7th Cavalry Regiment tried next and got to within half a mile of the dam before the stubborn defence of two Chinese companies halted their advance. There was limited artillery support for the attack due to poor roads and the division was suffering from low morale and was about to be pulled out of the line. The dam gates were eventually disabled in an attack by Navy Skyraider aircraft using torpedoes left over from the Second World War.

The 29th British Independent Brigade had taken up positions early in 1951 along the line of the Imjin River. The four infantry battalions – 1st Battalion, Royal Northumberland Fusiliers; 1st Battalion, the Gloucester Regiment; 1st Battalion, Royal Ulster Rifles and an attached Belgian battalion – had a nine-mile front to cover and would be spread very thinly. The enemy was nowhere to be found and fighting patrols were sent out across the river to look for them. They were there, but well hidden. The Chinese 63rd Army was waiting for the order to attack the British sector, destroy the brigade and push on to Seoul to cut off the UN forces to the east.

On the night of 22 April, the Chinese arrived at the river after a twenty-mile march in full battle order. As they began to wade across the 150 yard wide river, a patrol from the Glosters opened fire on them and began to call in mortar and artillery fire. When they ran low on ammunition the Glosters withdrew to Castle Hill and the Chinese assault began. For two days the brigade delayed the Chinese advance, but by the time their American commanders ordered their withdrawal it was too late. The Glosters were surrounded and eventually overrun, losing twenty dead, thirty-five wounded and 575 missing presumed captured. Their neighbouring battalions retreated in chaos, supported by the Centurion tanks of the 8th Hussars. The fighting was fierce. The tanks crushed the enemy under their tracks and swivelled their turrets to machine-gun the Chinese off each other's tanks. By the end of the day their armour ran red with the blood of the enemy. Sergeant Cadman found a Chinese man battering at his turret to get in, and drove his tank straight through the wall of a house, to brush him off, and then ran over a machine gun post at the side of the road. Some tanks left the road and took to the rice paddy and were ploughing-in Chinese infantrymen who were crouched under every bank. Very few of the British infantry-men clinging to the tanks, survived the hail of enemy fire.

The success of the Chinese offensive in breaching Line Kansas, led to a withdrawal of the whole Eighth Army to No Name Line, closer to Seoul. The fighting was extremely intensive and over a three day period of 24–26 April 1951, six American soldiers earned Medals of Honour, including four awarded to the 7th Infantry Regiment, 3rd Infantry Division. The rain hindered the Chinese advance, which petered out as it reached the new UN defensive positions, a mere six miles north of Seoul.

As April came to an end Van Fleet moved started moving his forces westwards, to reinforce the defences around the capital. This left the east of the country defended by X Corps and the ROK III Corps, a fact that did not go unnoticed by the Chinese. From 10–16 May they moved five armies eastward and launched an attack across the Soyang River against four ROK divisions. X Corps withdrew the ROK 5th and 7th Divisions under its command, but the ROK III Corps failed to do the same with its 3rd and 9th Divisions and the Chinese quickly destroyed both divisions and poured through the gap in the line. The Chinese had skilfully aimed their main offensive at the village of Namjon, which marked the boundary between the ROK 7th and 9th Divisions and between the US X Corps and the ROK III Corps. By nightfall they had severed the road which supplied the two divisions of III Corps and were preparing to attack III Corps from both the front and the rear.

Faced with a fight to the death or withdrawal, the two divisions chose the latter course of action. They discarded their trucks and artillery and fled south on foot through the Pangdae Mountains. Reports reached the neighbouring ROK I Corps that many personnel abandoned their personal weapons while officers ripped off their insignia of rank in case they were captured. The collapse of III Corps forced a huge bulge in the UN line and the US 3rd Infantry Division in reserve was rushed over a hundred miles to plug the gap. As a result of this debacle all ROK divisions were now attached to American Corps, with the exception of the three divisions of I Corps, now commanded by the recently promoted General Paik Sun Yup. ROK Army Headquarters was now limited to personnel, administrative, logistical and training matters and was no longer involved in operations.

The deployment of the US 3rd Infantry Division from Seoul to cover the retreat of the ROK III Corps and the orderly withdrawal of the ROK I Corps helped halt the communist advance. It was to be the last major Chinese offensive of the war and it failed, like most of the others due to a combination of heavy casualties and poor resupply. General Van Fleet recognized that the Chinese were exhausted and ordered a counter-attack. The goal was to regain the better defensive positions of Line Kansas north of the 38th Parallel and inflict maximum casualties on the enemy. They managed to encircle the 180th Division of the 60th Army and after days of hard fighting, broke up the division and the regiments fled in all directions. Soldiers either deserted or were abandoned by their officers and 5,000 prisoners were taken. The division commander and other officers who escaped were subsequently demoted back in China. By the time the mud and the rain had brought the counter-attack to an end 17,000 POWs had been taken by the UN forces, representing 80 per cent of the total Chinese POWs taken during the whole war.

By 10 June 1951 both sides had come to a halt and were taking up defensive positions roughly along the line of the 38th Parallel, from where the war had begun a year earlier. The Air Force then began Operation Strangle, a massive effort to destroy the Communist supply lines by air. On 23 June the Soviet ambassador to the UN called for cease-fire negotiations. The US Secretary of State Dean Acheson indicated US willingness to accept a cease-fire line in the vicinity of the 38th Parallel and on 2 July the Chinese and North Koreans finally agreed to begin negotiations at Kaesong, a village north of the front line in enemy territory. However, two more years would pass before they came to a conclusion.

Members of the Turkish Brigade move into position in December 1950, shortly after suffering severe casualties attempting to block the encirclement of the US 2nd Division at the Chongchon River in North Korea.

Korean refugees crossing the frozen Han River in January 1951. Advancing North Koreans dressed in civilian clothing often mingled with refugees to infiltrate behind the UN lines.

January 1951 the evacuation of Seoul is complete and engineers destroy a pontoon bridge across the Han River.

A Sherman tank from the last unit to evacuate Seoul crosses a pontoon bridge over the Han River just before it was destroyed to prevent it falling into communist hands.

Army engineers rig explosive satchel charges linked by primer cord to destroy this railway bridge.

3 January 1951, the 19th Regiment of the US 24th Infantry Division retreat ten miles south of Seoul.

Happy Valley, the area was the scene of the destruction of the tanks of Cooper Force and heavy casualties for the Royal Ulster Rifles in January 1951.

27 January 1951, Corporal Cliff Rodgers comes across the frozen bodies of civilians, shot with their hands bound behind their backs near Yangji, fifteen miles north-west of Inchon.

A bulldozer clears the road for a convoy to travel over a mountain pass north of Punggyi. The tank in the ditch is an earlier M4A3 105mm Sherman without a bulldozer blade and with the older vertical volute suspension system.

A machine gun crew from the US 25th Infantry Division keep watch for the enemy in January 1951.

29 February 1951 Canadian infantry taking a break to catch up with the news.

Some thirty kilometres south of Seoul – Chinese troops defending a ridgeline. Note the Czech-built ZB vz 26 LMG – the ancestor of the Bren – captured from Nationalist Chinese stocks.

A staged photograph of Chinese troops flushing American soldiers from a cave in the hillside.

White phosphorous shells fall on Chinese positions facing the US 25th Infantry Division in February 1951.

30 March 1951, an American M4A3E8 76 W (HVSS) tank fitted with a flame thrower destroys an enemy pillbox in the hillside on the Han River front.

Turkish troops searching captured Chinese soldiers. When the Turks first went into action they mistook retreating South Korean troops for the enemy and killed many of them. The Turkish forces, composed mainly of tough country boys who had, for the most part, never before left their villages, gained a fearsome reputation in close combat and rarely showed mercy to their foes, so much so that only about 100 were taken prisoner by the communists. Their brave defensive actions saved the US 2nd Division from annihilation.

A wounded man is prepared for evacuation in the side pannier carried by this OH-13 to a Mobile Army Surgical Hospital (MASH).

A new weapon for the UN forces to deal with: Chinese rocket salvoes. Communist rocket artillery was used to good effect during the defeat of the 8th Cavalry Regiment at Unsan.

South Korean Police
executing political prisoners
near Taegu in April 1951.

Chinese soldiers captured
near the Hwachon reservoir
fifty miles north-east of Seoul
in April 1951 await shipment
at the US 24th Infantry
Division headquarters.

A wrecked Cromwell tank of the 8th Hussars is recovered after the battle of Happy Valley. Its crew were either killed or captured. One of the few survivors saw captured tankmen executed in cold blood by their Chinese captors. The Chinese captured one of the Cromwells early in 1951 and it had to be knocked out by Centurion tanks several days later. The damage illustrates how destructive enemy infantry armed with explosives can be if they can get close enough to a tank.

A Chinese soldier has his photograph taken on a knocked-out M26 Pershing tank of the 1st Cavalry Division in the early months of the Chinese intervention.

June 1951 a British Mk III Centurion tank, painted with US markings runs off the road north of Seoul. A difficult recovery job for the men of the Royal Electrical and Mechanical Engineers. The Centurion's 20-pdr gun (the most powerful tank gun used in Korea) was renowned for its accuracy in destroying enemy bunkers, but never met the T-34 in combat in Korea. Note the failed HE penetrations on the side skirts.

A crippled American M4A3E8 76 W (HVSS) Sherman tank is prepared for recovery in October 1951. Note the 'A' frame attached to the rear of the tank ready for towing. These men from the 25th Infantry Division are placing dynamite under the track to split it so the tank can be towed.

A column of 1st Cavalry Division prisoners of war is escorted by armed guards on their long journey to the communist prison camps in the far north of Korea. Hundreds would perish on these long arduous marches without food or medical attention.

Large numbers of South Korean troops were captured by the Chinese who generally attacked the weaker ROK Divisions rather than the American units with their tanks, artillery and air support.

Chinese troops running through the streets of P'yongyang as the UN forces retreat south towards the 38th Parallel.

Chinese troops fighting their way through P'yongyang on the way to the south.

Chinese troops crossing the Han River under fire.

14 March 1951 American troops crowd onto a 1st Cavalry Division tank M4A3E8 76 W (HVSS) Sherman tank for a ride across the Hongchon River. The Sherman and Soviet T-34 were comparable and could destroy each other when hit. The Sherman had better optics however, which gave it a better chance of scoring a first round hit.

Chinese sniper Zhang Taofang claimed 214 UN dead in thirty-two days with his Mosin Nagant 7.62mm rifle.

A Marine sniper and his spotter search for targets in the valley below.

A Marine mortar crew firing their M2 4.2-inch heavy mortar from a well constructed dugout. The weapon had an effective range of 4,000 yards.

Men of the 14th Combat Engineer Battalion return fire at the communist forces across the river.

The Great Bug Out. UN troops crossing the 38th Parallel back into South Korea.

A temporary railway bridge is destroyed to prevent its use by the enemy during the retreat to the south.

February 1951, men of the 5th Regimental Combat Team at the Han River. This soldier is firing his Browning BAR whilst taking cover behind a M4A3E8 76 W (HVSS) Sherman tank. Note the large amount of MG ammunition stowed on the hull rear.

A forward observer team calls artillery fire onto an enemy position.

An interpreter with the Canadian Princess Patricias Light Infantry questions a Chinese prisoner.

Platoon leader Lieutenant Ralph Barnes throws a grenade as the enemy get closer.

A female Chinese medic tends to a wounded soldier as his comrades advance up the hill.

Major General Charles Palmer leads tanks of the 1st Cavalry Division through Chunchon on 21 March 1951.

Soldiers from the British Gloucestershire Regiment stop for afternoon tea. In April 1951 this battalion was overrun by a massive Chinese offensive and most of the men were taken prisoner.

April 1951, the Chinese launch their Fifth Offensive. Note the captured American trucks and 105mm artillery driving past. The photo also shows the use of good camouflage and concealment by Chinese soldiers to avoid UN air strikes and artillery.

A Chinese machine gun crew fire across the Imjin River in April 1951.

Chinese troops assaulting across the Imjin River. Their objective was the recapture of Seoul.

Chinese infantry assaulting a hill. Their human wave tactics were costly in manpower but very effective.

An 8-inch howitzer opens fire north of Seoul in May 1951 as UN troops move up behind withdrawing Chinese. The gun had a crew of fourteen and an effective range of 18,000 yards.

7 May 1951, a Marine uses his flame thrower to destroy an enemy pillbox.

April 1951, Chinese prisoners trudge down a hill under escort as UN troops advance past them.

Hongchon, 15 May 1951, Marines take cover while an M26 Pershing tank engages a target further down the valley.

May 1951, South Korean refugees queue to cross the Han River by a pontoon bridge hastily constructed alongside the railway bridge, whose destroyed piers can be seen in the distance.

The peace talks finally began in July 1951 at Kaesong, just north of the 38th Parallel and in enemy occupied territory. Communist guards surrounded the area to ensure the safety of the negotiators.

The burnt uniform on this dead Chinese infantryman is still smoking at this collection point near Chunchon on 17 May 1951 after UN forces halted a major enemy offensive.

A mine clearing party sweeping a main road in June 1951, escorted by an M4A3E8 76 W (HVSS) Sherman tank.

13 July 1951, Chinese tank crews stand in front of their camouflaged T-34 tanks before the start of the Fifth Chinese Offensive.

The Chinese would use human wave tactics to overrun a position, with inexperienced, poorly equipped soldiers in the first waves. Once the defenders began to run out of ammunition the following waves of well equipped veterans would join the battle. In the meantime other units would encircle the defenders and cut off their line of retreat or reinforcement. Note the supporting T-34 tanks.

This wounded GI was hit in the back in a grenade duel in July 1951.

The Chinese had little in the way of anti-aircraft weapons. This gunner is firing his Japanese made machine gun at a UN aircraft. The LMG is a type 96, which was based on the Czech ZB vz 26, the ancestor of the Bren.

General Matthew B. Ridgway (left), Far East Commander, confers with Brigadier Rockingham of the Canadian Army in July 1951.

August 1951, a US soldier
warily bypasses a booby
trapped Chinese roadblock
on a narrow mountain pass
near Ynaggu.

The caption supplied with
this propaganda photograph
reads 'A Chinese Peoples
Volunteer rescues a
wounded civilian'.

16 September 1951, an American soldier from the 2nd Engineer Special Brigade throws a hand grenade through the entrance to a Chinese bunker in the hillside.

20 September 1951, a Sikorsky H-19 drops elements of the 1st Marine Recon Company on Hill 812 to relieve troops from the 8th ROK Division.

Men of the Chinese 46th Army discuss tactics for their attack on Nanshan Village. Usually they would try to encircle enemy positions and establish road blocks on the line of retreat.

Waves of Chinese troops leave their trenches and hurl themselves into the valley below. By the autumn of 1951 the war on the ground had reached stalemate and both sides dug in to consolidate their positions.

A machine gun crew from Company K, 35th Regimental Combat Team, US 25th Infantry Division wait for the enemy to appear.

The Chinese 122nd Infantry Regiment prepares to go into battle. These men are armed with the Soviet PPSh 7.62mm submachine gun with a seventy-one-round drum magazine. The main tactic used in the assault was to equip one platoon with nothing but bags of grenades and another with sub machine guns.

North Korean dancers entertain Chinese troops behind the lines.

This photograph apparently shows a Chinese recoilless rifle crew destroying a UN tank. The US had provided the Nationalist Chinese the blueprints to manufacture the weapon and they fell into the hands of the Communists who produced their own version.

Royal Northumberland Fusiliers hitching a lift forward on a British Mk III Centurion tank. Note the US stars on the front and sides to aid identification. American gunners would often open fire on aircraft or vehicles that they did not recognize.

A unit from the 67th Chinese Army celebrates the capture of the 5th ROK battalion flag.

Wounded men from 'L' Company, 31st Infantry Regiment, US 7th Infantry Division take a smoke break after having their wounds dressed during the fighting for Hill 598 near Kumwha in October 1952.

Chinese troops celebrate victory at Triangle Hill. American and South Korean troops tried for forty-two days to capture the hill but were unsuccessful.

'A' Company, 31st Infantry Regiment prepare to defend their ridgeline. The regimental battle flag was captured by the Chinese in November 1950 and is now on display in the Peoples Military Museum in Beijing.

Chinese infantry from the 68th Army advancing towards the UN lines.

The members of this Chinese T-34 tank crew are presented with an award for their heroism. Although the Chinese had four tank regiments in North Korea, they were spread amongst the infantry units and tank to tank battles were rare.

Canadian Sherman M4A3E8 76 W (HVSS) tanks from C Squadron, Lord Strathcona's Horse crossing the Imjin River. Note the cover on the muzzle brake at the end of the gun barrel.

This Chinese photograph allegedly shows a raid by a dozen men from the 607th Regiment, 203rd Division, 68th Army Group on the headquarters of the South Korean White Tiger Regiment in July 1953. Led by Lieutenant Yang Yucai, deputy commander of the recon platoon and wearing South Korean uniforms, they caused heavy casualties and escaped with the Regimental flag.

A self-propelled M41 155mm Howitzer in action. Based on the M24 Chaffee light tank chassis, the gun had a range of 16,000 yards.

In October 1951 the 3rd Royal Australian Regiment captured Hill 317 from the 19th Chinese Division. The two Chinese soldiers nearest the camera are manning a Soviet DP light machine gun.

This is Bloody Ridge, occupied by the survivors of the 9th Infantry Regiment after it was captured on 5 September 1951. It cost 2,700 American and South Korean casualties and an estimated 15,000 North Korean casualties. The battle of Heartbreak Ridge, which followed Bloody Ridge, claimed 3,700 American and French casualties and an estimated 25,000 North Koreans and Chinese.

An Australian soldier armed with a Bren gun stands guard near the body of a North Korean soldier.

Wounded men from the US 2nd Division are carried to a first aid post during the fighting for Heartbreak Ridge.

11 October 1951, Colonel James Murray USMC senior US negotiator and Colonel Chang Chun San of the North Korean army study maps of the proposed cease-fire line at Panmunjom.

At the Panmunjom peace talks, DPRK delegation Deng Hua (third from left), Li Xiang-Chao (fourth from left), and Zhang Ping Chan (fifth from left).

In October 1951 Operation Polecharge was launched to seize a few hills south of the Wyoming Line, still held by the Communists. As a result of the six-mile advance the badly-mauled US 1st Cavalry Division was withdrawn to Japan for refitting.

Men of the 19th Infantry Regiment wait for the enemy counter attack to begin. Note the machine gun positioned to fire through the gap in the wall.

22 October 1951, prisoners of war from the 1st Commonwealth Division, captured during Operation Commando, a six division offensive against elements of four Chinese armies. It would be the last major UN offensive of the war.

Chapter Four

The Long Road to an Armistice

August 1951 – August 1953

Both sides now began to dig in and fortify their positions. The Chinese had learned to respect UN firepower and now conducted their operations at night. They were unable to use their traditional tactics of surrounding and outflanking the enemy; they would have to attack him head on and take heavy losses for their trouble. Their supply lines were now several hundred kilometres long and under attack by UN aircraft. According to the Chinese, UN forces dropped some 690,000 tons of bombs during the Korean War; five tons for every square kilometre in North Korea. The Chinese trucks had to operate at night, without lights on badly damaged roads; as a result the front line troops received only 30–40 per cent of their minimum needs. Although the Chinese had captured a large amount of UN heavy equipment and vehicles during the campaigns, most were destroyed immediately by UN aircraft. They had neither adequate air cover nor enough trained drivers to take the equipment away.

The peace talks began on 10 July 1951 at Kaesong, on the 38th Parallel but in Communist controlled territory. Vice-Admiral C. Turner Joy, commander of the US Naval Forces Far East was the chief US representative at the negotiations. He and the other four main members of the US team arrived by helicopter and took their seats opposite five negotiators representing China and North Korea, headed by General Nam Il. The Communist delegation had three proposals for consideration: a cease fire; the establishing of a demilitarized zone along the 38th Parallel; the withdrawal of all foreign forces from Korea. The American list contained nine items, including the identification of prisoner of war camps and access for the International Committee of the Red Cross. Arrangements would also have to be made for the exchange of prisoners of war.

The talks broke down after only two days. On 12 July the US delegation of sixty-five members arrived at the security entrance together with twenty journalists. As the presence of the journalists had not been agreed with the Communist delegation, they refused entrance to the journalists. As a result the Admiral and his team turned around and returned to their base at Munsan. It was an arrogant and needless act by the US side. The communists were prepared to agree to the presence of journalists, but only when some sort of agreement had been reached at the negotiating table.

Another source of dissatisfaction was the amount of security around Kaesong, through which the US delegation had to pass. General Ridgway had agreed to meet the communist representatives at Kaesong, but thereafter regretted the decision. These side issues kept both sides occupied until October.

By 26 July, both sides agreed to discuss the following five items:

1. Pass the agenda of the talks.
2. Determine the military demarcation line between the two sides in order to establish a nonmilitary zone. This would provide a foundation for the hostile actions in Korea to come to an end.
3. Arrange details for an effective cease-fire and armistice in Korea, including the organization, authority, and responsibilities of a committee supervising the implementation of the clauses concerning the cease-fire and armistice.
4. Exchange prisoners of war and civilian internees.
5. Propose items needed to be suggested to the governments related to the two parties.

The procedure for processing Chinese prisoners of war, as of August and September 1951, was to send them to a collecting point not far behind the front lines within twenty-four to forty-eight hours of their capture. The wounded would be given medical treatment, before being sent to hospitals at Pusan. The non-wounded prisoners were registered, tagged, deloused, given haircuts etc and kept at the collecting point for varying periods before being sent to Pusan. There they would stay for a few days to a month before being sent on to POW compounds on Koje-do, an island off the south coast of Korea.

At that time it appeared that few officers were being taken prisoner. It later became obvious that captured officers were claiming to be enlisted men and as they all wore the same uniform it was difficult to differentiate between the two. A major source of Chinese prisoners was the destruction of the 180th Division and the capture of 3,000 prisoners including the Division Commissar Pei Shan. His identity was revealed by one of the prisoners during an interrogation session and he was promptly hanged by his own side.

Many of the prisoners were remarkably forthcoming once their interrogations were under way. A captured Chinese soldier, Lee Zeu Win, prisoner of war number 704110 from the 579th Regiment, 193rd Division, 65th Army, claimed that on 8 May 1951, he and two unnamed others shot and killed two captured British prisoners in the vicinity of the Imjin River. The prisoners were not bound but were required to sit on the ground and were shot in the back. The bodies were not buried. A sketch was made of the place of execution.

Interrogation of the prisoners of war soon revealed that many of them were formerly members of the Chinese Nationalist Army who had been captured and impressed into the Communist Army. Many others were South Koreans who had been forced to join the North Korean Army. The decision facing the UN Command was whether to repatriate all of the prisoners of war, including those who did not wish to return home, or allow the men to decide themselves. The Allies had learnt a hard lesson at the end of the Second World War, when they forcibly repatriated tens of thousands of Russians who had surrendered to the Germans. Stalin had insisted on their return, so he could punish them for surrendering in the first place. Although not all of them had agreed to join the German Army in order to escape starvation in their prison camps, they were all shipped off to the Siberian prison camps as punishment; the officers were generally shot as soon as they set foot again on Russian soil. The ill-feeling that this created behind the Iron Curtain caused the supply of enemy defectors to dry up for some years after the end of the war. Why defect or surrender to the Americans if they only send you back to where you came from? If the Allies repeated this process in Korea, what effect would it have in a future war – would enemy soldiers be more reluctant to surrender if they knew they might be sent back for punishment at the end of the war?

It was decided to allow the prisoners of war to choose for themselves whether they wanted to return home or not. This angered the Communist delegation who demanded that all prisoners be sent home at the end of hostilities. This sticking point would delay the signing of an armistice for two more years and cause hundreds of thousands of casualties on both sides.

Perhaps there is another explanation for the Allied insistence on right of choice for the prisoners; they knew that not all UN prisoners of war would be returned at the end of the war. The CIA had discovered that at least two train loads of UN prisoners had been sent to the Soviet Union via China. The CIA source was at the railway station at Manchouli, near the border of Manchuria and Siberia when the first transfer took place late in 1951. He saw hundreds of men in American uniforms boarding a train en-route to Siberia. A large number of them were negroes. He went to the railway restaurant and observed three POWs who were under guard and were conversing in English. They wore sleeve insignia which indicated that they were Air Force non-commissioned officers. The CIA source, a Greek refugee who eventually left China through Hong Kong, observed a second train load of POWs in the spring of 1952. At no time did he see prisoners returning from Siberia. The Consulate General and the Assistant Air Liaison Officer at the Hong Kong consulate evaluated the information as 'probably true'.

The CIA received a number of reports during the war concerning UN prisoners of war held in China. One was dated 25 October 1951 and stated that local people had been forbidden to talk to American and British prisoners of war held in a compound at 52 Fu Hsing Road, Shanghai. The order was issued by a staff member of the Central and South China military area headquarters on 13 September and the prisoners included men from the US Eighth Army, the British Gloucester Regiment and the Argylls. The names included First Lieutenant Metcalf, Warrant Officer Booth and enlisted men Ross, Wright, Jarvis and Borden, none of whom ever returned home again.

It was clear that none of these men would never return. As far as the author can determine, the subject of men passed on to the Russians was never discussed at the peace talks and their return was not made a condition of the armistice. The Chinese and Russians had started the game of not returning prisoners; the United Nations would finish it.

The twelve months of bloody fighting had shown Mao Zedung, Joseph Stalin and Harry Truman that total victory was unattainable and could even lead to total war between the Communists and the West. General MacArthur was already advocating the use of nuclear weapons on the concentrations of Chinese troops, a frame of mind which would eventually lead to his dismissal.

As their political masters had decided to enter negotiations to end the war, the Generals of both sides were reluctant to engage in any major offensives while the talking progressed. They confined their activities to exchanges of artillery fire, raids and patrols and the occasional attempt to seize nearby hills to improve their defensive lines.

The first main stumbling block was the agreement of a cease-fire line. The Chinese wanted both sides to withdraw to the 38th Parallel, from which the war had initially begun. The Americans however, insisted on the cease-fire line being where the two sides were currently dug-in, because the terrain was easier to defend. The communists broke off the talks on 23 August and the fighting continued.

The UN forces had been trying to take over an area known as the Punchbowl, which served as an important Communist staging area. The fighting was concentrated around three interconnecting hills south-west of the Punchbowl known collectively as Bloody Ridge. Three days after the Communists walked out of the talks the ROK 7th Division captured the mountain after a week of heavy combat. The next day the North Koreans recaptured the mountain and held it against the best efforts of the US 2nd Infantry Division's 9th Infantry Regiment. Finally the Division commander ordered his units to outflank the mountain and the North Koreans pulled back on 5 September. The cost of the effort was approximately 15,000 North Koreans and 2,700 UN soldiers killed, wounded or captured.

On 25 October the UN and Communist negotiators resumed their discussions at a new location, a collection of tents in the village of Panmunjom, six miles east of Kaesong. The Communists agreed that the truce line should be based upon the current lines of contact, but in order to prevent them from ignoring the other issues, the Americans insisted that the proposed line be valid for only thirty days. The fighting would continue until all other issues had been resolved.

The main item of contention was the return of all prisoners of war, as required by the Geneva Convention. The Chinese and North Koreans insisted that all their men be returned, whereas the American position was that the Communist prisoners should have a choice as to whether or not they went home. It is quite ironic when one considers the fact that both China and Russia were sending UN prisoners of war to camps behind the Iron Curtain from which they would never return.

The UN prisoners of war in the Communist camps along the Yalu River were also being used as pawns in the negotiations. The Chinese were unprepared for the large numbers of prisoners of war and it was not until January 1951 that permanent camps were established to house them. In the meantime 40 per cent of the US prisoners had died from starvation, disease or neglect.

The Communists were not in a hurry to improve the conditions of the prisoners. They were less likely to make trouble or try to escape if they were weak and hungry. They then began to 'brainwash' their captives, by promising better food and conditions if they made anti-war or anti-American statements or broadcast Peace messages over Peking Radio. Many men pretended to go along with this coercion in order to stay alive, although some became genuine Progressives and came to embrace the Communist line. Some became members of the Central Committee of American and British Prisoners Promoting Peace and issued a letter in December 1951: 'To Peace-Loving Peoples of the World. We want to go home. Though the Chinese Peoples Volunteers treat us very well here, cooking good food and taking good care of us, we still miss our hometowns and families very badly etc'.

This favourable treatment was not being extended to the members of the Kennel Club, a punishment cell for Reactionaries in one of the Chinese prison camps. The kennels were boxes five feet long, less than four feet high and just wide enough for the occupant to lie on his back. The five boxes held Lance Corporal Mathews of the Glosters, Fusilier Derek Kinne of the Royal Northumberland Fusiliers and Americans 'Doc' McCabe, Tom Cabello and Sal Conte. McCabe was being punished for trying to reconvert prisoners who had fallen for the Chinese propaganda; Mathews was suspected of being a member of the escape committee and Kinne was probably one of the toughest of the lot. He had escaped with two others, but had been recaptured after struggling for eighteen miles with a rupture. Tom Cabello had also escaped and over nineteen days covered over 200 miles before he was recaptured, almost in sight of friendly lines. These men would be held in harsh conditions right until the end of the war.

In the UN prison camps near Pusan, screening had begun to determine which prisoners would like to stay and which ones would like to go home. Some 40,000 South Koreans who had been forced to fight for North Korea were reclassified as 'civilian internees' and would be eventually released in the South. The screening process aggravated tensions between the pro- and anti-Communist prisoners. There were now Communist agents in the camps who had deliberately allowed themselves to be captured and they fermented violent uprisings during the spring of 1952. These had to be suppressed by US paratroopers using tear gas and fixed bayonets.

In April 1952 UN officials announced that only 70,000 of the 170,000 civil and military prisoners then held by the United Nations wished to return home to North Korea and the Peoples Republic of China. This was of course unacceptable to the Communists who would clearly lose face and the talks became deadlocked.

In order to increase the pressure on the UN negotiators the pro-Communists, armed with a variety of home made weapons attempted to take control of the interior of the camps. In May they scored a stunning coup when they succeeded in capturing Brigadier General Francis Dodd, the commandant of the main POW camp on Koje-do, when he came too close to the compound gate as a Communist working party walked by. In order to secure his release the Americans pledged to suspend additional repatriation screenings in a poorly worded communiqué that appeared to substantiate Communist allegations that the UN had been mistreating prisoners. He was released and subsequently relieved of his command.

On the front lines, the grand offensives had been replaced by local raids and artillery duels. The Chinese had greatly increased their artillery strength with captured American weapons and equipment supplied by the Soviet Union. Some days up to 20,000 shells would be fired at the UN lines and the American gunners would respond ten-fold.

Atrocities continued to take place on the front lines during 1952. On 21 September an American artillery forward observer team and a squad of South Koreans were dug-in on Hill 854 near Samchi-yong. Their position was overrun by the enemy, but recaptured the following day. An affidavit made by the lieutenant who found the bodies of the two Americans read: 'One of the boys had no head. It seemed to have been mashed or beaten and was lying all over the road. Both of his feet had been cut off about half way between the knee and ankle. It appeared as though they had been chopped off with a dull instrument. The other GI had his eyes gouged out, and nothing remained where his eyes were except holes. He had been bayoneted all over the body with the upper parts of his legs completely laid open to the bone.' The bodies of the South Koreans had received similar treatment, one of them having had the genitals severed with a sharp instrument — they were lying alongside the corpse.

When the peace talks stalled again on 8 October, General Van Fleet decided to increase the pressure on the battlefield and gave the order to capture the Triangle Hill mountain complex three miles north of Kumhwa. He was confident that two infantry battalions, with sufficient support, should be able to capture Triangle Hill and its neighbour Sniper ridge in five days with about 200 casualties. He could not have been more wrong. Despite 200 fighter bomber sorties and the support of nearly 300 artillery guns the Chinese could not be moved. He threw one battalion in after another and the US 7th Infantry Division and the ROK 2nd Division suffered over 9,000 casualties in a futile attempt to take the mountain. Chinese casualties were estimated at over 19,000, but they had plenty more men to take their place. The United States did not and after all, it was an election year.

In January 1953 Dwight D. Eisenhower succeeded Harry S. Truman as President of the United States. A former five-star General with his reputation made in Europe during the Second World War, his election caused uncertainty amongst the Communist leaders. Although he had campaigned on a platform of ending the war, he might well have decided to do so by winning it.

On 13 December 1952, the Executive Committee of the League of Red Cross Societies, meeting in Geneva, adopted a resolution proposed by the Indian delegate that recommended the sick and wounded prisoners be exchanged prior to a truce. The proposal was put directly to the Communists in February 1953, but no reply was received. However, on 5 March, Joseph Stalin died and China and North Korea realized they could make their own decisions without looking over their shoulders towards Moscow. On 28 March, the Communists not only agreed to exchange some sick and wounded prisoners, but also proposed a resumption of the truce negotiations which had been suspended six months previously.

The exchange took place in April 1953 at Panmunjom, where the Communist ambulances would drive to a chalk line fronting a series of reception tents. The sick and wounded were counted and a receipt given for their delivery. A brief medical check followed to ascertain whether the returning prisoner was strong enough for the forty-five minute ambulance ride to Freedom Village, or whether he should be taken by helicopter. There were two Freedom Villages, one each for returning ROK prisoners and for American and UN prisoners. They were huge compounds with processing and hospital tents. General Mark Clark, the Commander in Chief of the United Nations Command, was there to welcome each of the 149 American prisoners home.

A total of 684 UN prisoners were returned, including 32 British and in exchange 6,670 North Koreans and Chinese were sent home. It later transpired that an additional 234 sick and wounded US and UN prisoners and 141 South Korean prisoners who were eligible for repatriation, were kept back by the Communists.

Unfortunately, the Chinese were not playing by the rules. Instead of repatriating the most sick or injured of their prisoners, they sent back lightly wounded to appear to the world that they had been treating the men well. They also returned many prisoners who were sympathetic to the Communist cause – so-called 'progressives'. However, it was a start.

The prisoners who came back during 'Little Switch' were questioned and had much to report about death marches and the conditions in the enemy prisoner of war camps. It was estimated that on one of the six main death marches, from Tokch'on to Death Valley in the eastern province of North Korea, between 200 and 800 of the prisoners died or were killed on the march. The death rates in the prisoner of war camps were equally shocking. Between 3,000 and 6,000 men died of their wounds or starvation or were deliberately killed. At Camp 5 at least 1,800 died and are buried on the hills surrounding the camp on the border with China.

While the news of the deaths of prisoners in enemy hands was new to the UN Command, the subject of war crimes and atrocities was not. By the end of June 1953, the War Crimes Division files held details of 1,615 alleged atrocity cases. The majority, 1,134 took place in South Korea and 478 in North Korea. The files revealed that the North Korean Peoples Army was responsible for 1,164 of the atrocities and the Chinese Communist Forces were instigators of 439. The perpetrators of a dozen other cases were still to be identified.

As many as 57,000 people, both civilian and military were reportedly killed in these atrocities and the bodies of 10,032 had been recovered, as well as 533 survivors who provided proof of these acts. As far as the author can ascertain, no war crimes trials were ever held. Some of the perpetrators had been captured and had admitted their participation in war crimes. However, some were repatriated during 'Little Switch' and others would disappear in mass break outs from the POW camps in June 1953.

The final four months before the ceasefire was agreed saw one crisis after another. In May 1953 the Communists gave such indications of bad faith and evasiveness that General Clark was authorized by Washington to terminate the talks and continue the war. All the while South Korean President Syngman Rhee was threatening to derail the peace talks. Not only was Korea still divided in two, but he now had over a million Chinese facing him across the 38th Parallel.

Finally, it was agreed that any prisoners who did not want to return home would be handed over to representatives from India – a neutral country, where they would remain for ninety days while their governments subjected them to 'explanations' and tried to persuade them to come home. At the end of ninety days they would revert to civilian status and the neutral commission would help them to relocate to a new home. South Korean President Rhee did not agree with this though; as far as he was concerned, on the day the armistice was to be signed any North Korean who did not want to return home would be set free to live in the South. He went even further on the night of 18 June when the ROK guards at the four main POW camps threw open the gates and the first of 25,000 North Koreans who did not want to be repatriated walked out into the night. They were met by ROK soldiers and police and given civilian clothes and directions to private houses where they would be taken care of.

The Chinese reaction was swift and violent. They launched their heaviest offensive in over two years and fired so many artillery rounds at the UN lines that they used up most of the shells they had stockpiled during that time. They then threw three Chinese armies totalling 100,000 men against five ROK divisions of less than half that number and pushed them back several miles until UN artillery and air support stalled the offensive. The fighting continued into the early days of July and clearly shook President Rhee's determination to continue the war without UN support.

The armistice was finally signed on 27 July 1953, and on 5 August 'Operation Big Switch' began with the first exchange of prisoners of war from both sides desiring repatriation. The United Nations Command began the transfer of 75,823 enemy prisoners of war (70,183 North Koreans and 5,640 Chinese) and the communists began the transfer of 12,773 Allied prisoners including 7,862 South Koreans, 3,597 Americans and 1,000 British in return.

It soon became clear that the numbers did not add up. On 6 August the Commander in Chief of the United Nations Command, General Mark Clark, flew back to the United States and held a news conference in the Pentagon. The *New York Times* reported his concerns that the Communists were holding back a large number of prisoners: 'General Clark pledged to press the communists for further information on the additional troops he believed they held and for a possible exchange. He said that he pointed out the wide discrepancy between his information and that supplied by the communists on prisoners during the truce negotiations. He had been advised by his superiors in the Pentagon, he said, not to delay the armistice negotiations over the discrepancy but to reserve the privilege of later protest.'

General Clark was of the opinion that the only way of obtaining the release of all missing prisoners of war was by the application of force and in that respect his hands were tied. It was with great reluctance that he announced at the press conference that he would retire from the army on 31 October 1953. His opinion was echoed the following day by General James A. Van Fleet, commander of the Eighth Army, when he stated: 'A large percentage of the 8,000 American soldiers listed as missing in action in Korea are still alive.'

Almost 3,000 American prisoners of war had died or been killed whilst in captivity – 38 per cent of the total of 7,190 captured. However, there were hundreds, if not thousands more who were being kept back as the exchanges were under way. Returned prisoners told stories of comrades who were taken away from their waiting areas and never seen again. This was in addition to the many intelligence reports of

American and UN prisoners being taken across the Yalu River into China and the train loads of prisoners seen crossing the Manchurian frontier into Russia.

On 6 September both sides declared that 'Big Switch' had been completed for all individuals who had elected to return home to their own sides. Three days later the UNC presented a list to the Communists of 3,404 UN and South Korean personnel who were still not accounted for. The list included the names of 944 United States servicemen and was compiled from statements made by the communists themselves, propaganda radio broadcasts made from Peking, letters written from POW camps or from the observations of repatriated comrades. On 16 December Peking radio stated that the list was fake and designed to obscure the fact that the Allies were forcibly detaining Chinese and North Korean prisoners of war. At this point an impasse was reached. The UN Command now knew that the enemy was holding back some prisoners and had no intention of returning them. On the other hand the fact that tens of thousands of communist soldiers had refused to return home was of enormous political value. The communists had a small victory of their own in that twenty-one Americans and one British Royal Marine refused to return home, as well as over 300 South Koreans. However, 22,604 Chinese and North Koreans were handed over to the Indian delegation of the Neutral Nations Repatriation Commission on 23 September, having turned their backs on their communist masters. When added to the 25,000 North Koreans Rhee had freed in June, it meant that over 46,000 Communist soldiers had refused repatriation.

Was it worth it? After the negotiators at Panmunjom had agreed the cease-fire line in November 1951, the repatriation question was the only substantial issue left. By insisting on voluntary repatriation the United States had prolonged the war by fifteen months, during which 125,000 United Nations and over 250,000 Communist soldiers had become casualties.

By the time the guns fell silent for the last time, the United States had lost 23,196 killed in action and a further 105,871 wounded. A total of 13,108 had been listed as missing in action, although 5,131 had returned during the prisoner exchanges. Nearly 8,000 were still listed as missing in action and although many may have died or been killed, there were at least 944 others who had been alive in enemy hands at one time or another.

The armistice was never replaced by a formal peace treaty and technically both North and South Korea are still at war. A demilitarized zone was established between both countries and it has been transformed into the heaviest defended place in the world. The Chinese troops eventually marched back into China and most of the UN forces returned home, leaving a strong force of American troops to help the South Koreans patrol the frontier between the two countries.

And so the years have passed. The last ten years have seen the return of a number of former ROK soldiers who were kept back at the end of the war and sent to work in coal mines in North Korea. As a succession of famines have ravaged North Korea, so have refugees crossed the Yalu River into China and made their way back to South Korea.

In the last year or so the North Koreans have torpedoed a South Korean war ship and shelled a coastal village in response to US naval exercises in the area. The North is also reportedly in possession of a handful of nuclear weapons and is working hard to produce an inter-continental ballistic missile to carry the warheads. Peace is as far away as ever.

Chinese 85mm anti-aircraft artillery was positioned throughout the North in order to protect their supply lines from UN bombers.

Two Chinese sentries stand guard on the edge of the neutral zone at Panmunjom, midway between the communist and UN lines, where the two year truce talks were largely held. Chinese sentries were also positioned on hilltops to give advance warning to supply convoys of approaching American aircraft.

The Freedom Gate bridge over the Imjin River was built by the 84th Engineer Construction Battalion. The original was destroyed by bombs on 10 March 1952.

Enemy 82mm mortar bombs exploding on Marine ridgeline trenches on 8 April 1952.

April 1953, a North Korean supply train is hit by napalm dropped by a B-26 as it waits in the marshalling yards.

The 90mm M2 gun had a dual role, functioning as an anti-tank as well as an anti-aircraft gun. The gun could fire up to twenty-four rounds per minute due to its upgraded ammunition feed and automatic fuse setter/rammer. The gun was not ideal in the anti-tank role due to its high silhouette and more complicated sights.

Chinese coastal artillery positioned to prevent further amphibious landings by UN forces. These are ex-Soviet 76mm divisional guns of Second World War vintage.

Marines firing their towed 4.5-inch multiple-barrelled rocket launcher towards enemy lines. One drawback was the dust and debris kicked up by the backblast, which soon identified the location of the Marines to enemy spotters.

A platoon from the 3rd Ranger Company, US 3rd Infantry Division prepare for a night patrol. Their objective would be to try to snatch a prisoner.

UN troops watch with interest as artillery shells fall on communist positions across the valley.

When the front lines stabilized the Chinese dug extensive fortifications, sometimes extending up to twenty miles behind their lines.

Marines on Siberia Hill watch the results of artillery fire in the distance. Their turn would come on the night of 8 August 1952 when the Chinese launched an assault on the hill.

A Marine OH-13 helicopter lands at a Mobile Army Surgical Hospital with wounded carried in its two side panniers.

British prisoners of war playing a soccer game at Chongsong prisoner of war camp. Prisoners of the communists were either classed as reactionaries or progressives. The reactionaries would receive harsh treatment in separate camps; progressives would receive lenient treatment, especially if their activities reflected well upon their captors.

The aftermath of a failed human wave assault, defeated by US artillery.

This huge pile of artillery shell casings was created in June 1953 after four days of fighting for Outpost Henry. It was very difficult for the arms factories in America to keep up with the rate of useage and the empty casings were shipped home to speed up the process. Empty shell cases were routinely salvaged where possible for re-use or to at least recycle the metal to lower costs.

Chinese mortar round exploding on top of a US Marine position. Note the rifles stacked to the left of the trench. One would have thought that their owners would have had them in their hands in case an assault was about to follow the mortar barrage.

The site of the peace talks at Panmunjom with an H-19 helicopter parked nearby.

US Air Force B-26 bombers drop napalm on an enemy supply collection point near Hanchon, North Korea. These attacks were just as likely to kill civilians as soldiers.

With both sides dug in and camouflaged in fortified positions it was left to the Air Force and long-range artillery to take the fight to the enemy.

This was an enormous propaganda victory for the Chinese who staged this inter-camp prisoner of war 'Olympics' in November 1952. Improved food and living conditions played a big part in the decision of the prisoners to co-operate.

A Chinese gunner firing his water-cooled machine gun from the top of a ridge. The Chinese were so well dug-in that UN artillery fire was hard pressed to shift them.

This soldier is firing an M18 57mm recoilless rifle. It was very useful against enemy machine gun nests and three were issued to each rifle company. Copies of the M18 were produced by the Chinese as the Type 36. It had an effective range of 490 yards and a maximum range of over two miles.

March 1953, a US forward observation post overlooking Old Baldy west of Chorwon. The battles that took place at this stage of the war were a futile waste of lives, while the negotiations over prisoners dragged on.

A machine gun crew gives supporting fire to UN troops. The soldier on the left has two ammunition magazines tapes back to back for quicker changing when faced with hordes of charging infantry.

The prisoner of war camps on Koje-do island contained pro-Communist Chinese and North Koreans as well as anti-Communist Chinese and South Koreans impressed into the North Korean Army. Violent riots broke out between the various factions.

24 April 1953, Operation Little Switch begins with the exchange of sick and wounded prisoners of war. The Chinese actually sent back fit men who had shown sympathy with the communist cause, while hundreds of more deserving cases remained behind.

Chinese and North Korean prisoners of war leave their compound for the first exchange of sick and wounded prisoners of war in April 1953.

May 1953, a Sikorsky S-19 from the 6th Transportation Helicopter Company delivers rations for members of the 35th Infantry Regiment, US 25th Infantry Division near Panmunjom.

July 1953, Operation Big Switch begins and a convoy of Chinese prisoners of war head for home.

Chinese volunteers celebrating the end of the war.

The Chinese Peoples Volunteers begin to return home.

Some of the twenty Americans who decided to remain behind in North Korea. They were joined by one British Royal Marine. Most eventually returned to their homeland.

Notes

Notes

Notes

Notes

Notes

Notes

Notes

Notes

Notes